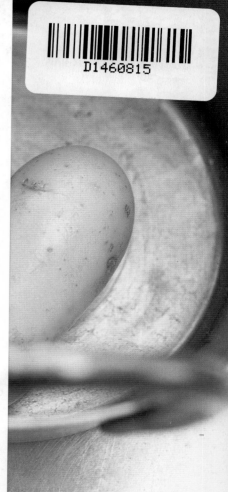

a passion for potatoes

a passion for potatoes

Paul Gayler

with photography by Gus Filgate

KYLE CATHIE LIMITED

to my wife, anita, and to my
Late mothers, LiLian and joyce

First published in Great Britain in 2001 by
Kyle Cathie Limited, 23 Howland Street, London W1T 4AY

ISBN 978 1 85626 949 0

Text © 2001 Paul Gayler   Photography © 2001 Gus Filgate

Project editor Sheila Boniface • Editor Jane Middleton • Designer Heidi Baker
Home economist Linda Tubby • Stylist Penny Markham

Paul Gayler is hereby identified as the author of this work in accordance with
Section 77 of the Copyright, Designs and Patents Act 1988.

A CIP catalogue record for this title is available from the British Library.

Printed and bound in Singapore by Tien Wah Press

contents

INtRODUCtION

What other vegetable evokes such nostalgic feelings as the potato? It is part and parcel of my childhood memories – roast potatoes for Sunday lunch; baked potatoes thrown on the fire on Guy Fawkes Night; a midweek supper of sausage and mash; and, of course, fish and chips on a Friday. My particular passion was mashed potatoes with salad cream, which I have to admit I still enjoy but I like to feel that my tastes have widened a little since then!

When I was a child it was hard to imagine a meal without potatoes. Since then, we've embraced pasta and rice enthusiastically and we no longer expect to see potatoes on our plate every day. But they're still one of the most popular vegetables, and no wonder. Potatoes are astonishingly versatile, lending themselves to just about every cooking method, from baking, boiling, steaming, roasting and frying to use in breads, pies, cakes and puddings. And it's good to see that there has been a revival of interest in old-fashioned potato varieties recently, plus the development of some exciting new ones. Gone are the days when the greengrocer asked, 'Reds or whites, love?' Now we can choose from a range that includes knobbly Pink Fir Apple, yellow-fleshed Yukon Gold, and the mysterious purple-black truffle potatoes. Like all good things, potatoes can be endlessly reinvented while never losing their essential character. Food trends may come and go but I suspect the humble spud will never be out of fashion.

a SHORt HISTORY Of tHe potato

Life without the potato is almost unthinkable (no mash, no chips …) but in fact it is a relative newcomer to Europe and North America. Now one of our culinary staples, it very nearly didn't become established at all.

Potatoes have been cultivated in Peru since at least 200BC but it wasn't until the early sixteenth century that Spanish Conquistadors took them to Europe, where they were regarded, alongside tomatoes and aubergines, as the work of the devil. They were also believed to be poisonous, which is not so surprising when you consider that they belong to the same family as deadly nightshade.

In 1589, Sir Walter Raleigh introduced the potato to Ireland, when he planted seeds on a 40,000-acre plot near Cork given to him by Queen Elizabeth I. He neither liked nor understood potatoes though, and eventually ordered them to be uprooted. In France, too, they were unpopular, until Antoine Parmentier convinced Louis XVI that they could bring an end to famine. He organised court banquets with potatoes in every course, and persuaded Marie

Antoinette to wear potato blossoms in her hair and have them embroidered into her evening gowns, thus ensuring that they became fashionable. Meanwhile, in Prussia, Frederick the Great had recognised the potato's potential as a food source and distributed seeds to the peasantry, along with instructions for cultivation and a warning to any who objected that their nose would be cut off if they failed to comply!

Eventually the adaptability of the potato to all manner of soils, climates and cultures made it a staple ingredient throughout the world, particularly in Europe and America. Its crucial role in sustaining entire populations became apparent in 1845, when potato blight hit Europe. This deadly fungus destroyed crops for several years in succession and had an enormous political impact, contributing to general unrest and sowing the seeds of revolution and immigration. Arguably the consequences are still with us today. In Ireland, where the potato had become a major food source, the disaster hit particularly hard. Nearly one and a half million people died, large numbers emigrated, and the country took many years to recover.

In 1995, potatoes became the first vegetable to be grown in space. Today, they remain a major food source, playing a vital role in many cuisines. They are no longer seen as food for the poor; instead, unusual varieties are attractively packaged and sold at a premium price.

The recipes in this book are a tribute to the versatility of potatoes and the affection with which they are regarded throughout the world. If there is a message it is simply this: be adventurous and eat more potatoes!

potatoes are good for us

Contrary to popular belief, potatoes are packed with goodness. They are not fattening, although very often their accompaniments are (butter, cream, cheese, oil …). Plainly cooked potatoes contain only 87 kilocalories per 100g. Even when roasting or frying potatoes, it is possible to minimise the amount of fat they absorb by making sure the butter or oil is very hot before adding the potatoes.

Here are just some of the health benefits of potatoes:

- They are high in starchy carbohydrate, making them a good source of energy (experts recommend we should increase our intake of starchy carbohydrate foods such as potatoes, bread, pasta and rice).
- They are high in potassium, which helps to counteract the adverse effects of salt in our diet.
- They contain a useful amount of vitamin C (about 10mg per 100g baked potato). The vitamin C content is highest in newly harvested potatoes and decreases during storage and prolonged cooking, or if the potatoes are left to soak in water before cooking.
- They also contain iron and vitamins B1 (thiamin) and B2 (riboflavin).
- They contain no cholesterol and virtually no fat and are low in sodium.

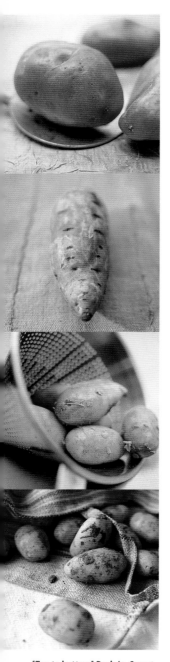

[Top to bottom] Desirée, Sweet,
Jersey Royal, Nicola

the most nutritious way to cook potatoes

The most nutritious way to cook potatoes is in their skins, since most of the vitamins and minerals lie in or just beneath the skin. Baking potatoes in their jackets, therefore, is an ideal way of preserving all the nutrients. Boiling potatoes in their skins has a dual advantage: not only does it prevent the vitamins leaching out into the cooking water but it also ensures that the potatoes hold their shape better.

Throughout this book you will notice that some recipes call for the potatoes to be peeled while in others they are left unpeeled; it is really a matter of personal taste. If you do peel potatoes, peel them as thinly as possible just before cooking. Always boil them in the smallest amount of water and never leave them in hot water after cooking.

CHOOSING the RIGHT potato

There are some 4,000 varieties of potato available worldwide at present, and even though only a tiny fraction of these appears in the shops there is understandably some confusion about which potatoes are best for which cooking methods.

With just a few exceptions, potatoes can be divided into two main categories:
- Floury potatoes (sometimes called mealy potatoes) are high in starch and have a low water content. This is because the sugar has been converted to starch by the time the potato is harvested. These potatoes become fluffy when cooked, making them suitable for roasting, baking, mashing and chips. They are not good for boiling, unless you intend to mash them, because they break up.
- Waxy potatoes are low in starch but have a high water content. They usually have a firm texture and a shiny appearance. They keep their shape when cooked, making them suitable for salads or any other occasion when you want to serve them whole. They are also good for sautéing and gratins.

However, this is not the only means of classification. Potatoes can also be categorised according to their age:
- New potatoes (earlies) are traditionally planted early in the year and are available in late spring and early summer. However, modern methods of cultivation mean that 'new' potatoes are now imported from other countries throughout the winter – although arguably the flavour of the first homegrown ones is best. Most new potatoes are waxy varieties. When cooking new potatoes, you should add them to boiling salted water rather than putting them in cold water.
- Old potatoes (maincrop) are mainly floury varieties, which have been left in the ground until fully grown and then harvested in the autumn. Unlike new potatoes, they keep well and can be stored for several months in optimum conditions. Old potatoes should be put in cold water and brought to the boil rather than added to boiling water, as this makes them less likely to break up during cooking.

In other countries, such as the US, potatoes are classified by their shape and the colour of their skin or flesh – hence recipes calling for red, yellow, russet or white potatoes.

Below is a guide to the more popular varieties of potatoes and their uses, but let's not forget that whatever the ideal variety for each dish, you can of course choose any potato you like – as long as you bear in mind that the end result will be slightly different. For example, using waxy potatoes instead of floury ones to make mash will give a more glutinous texture. Different potato varieties all have their own characteristics and part of the pleasure of cooking with potatoes is experimenting to find out what you like best.

top of the crops

Floury potatoes	Steaming/boiling	Salads	Mashing	Roasting	Shallow-frying	Deep-frying	Baking
Cara				●		●	●
Estima	●					●	
Golden Wonder		●	●		●	●	
Home Guard	●						
Kerrs Pink	●		●	●			
King Edward			●	●		●	●
Marfona	●						●
Maris Piper			●	●		●	●
Pentland Crown						●	
Pentland Dell			●	●		●	●
Pentland Squire						●	
Red Pontiac	●			●			
Romano			●	●		●	●
Russet Burbank		●			●	●	
Santé			●				●
Truffle potatoes	●	●	●	●			
Wilja	●		●			●	●
Yukon Gold		●	●			●	●

Waxy potatoes	Steaming/boiling	Salads	Mashing	Roasting	Shallow-frying	Deep-frying	Baking
Belle de Fontenay	●	●			●		
Bintje				●	●	●	
Carlingford	●	●		●			
Charlotte	●	●			●		
Desiree			●	●		●	●
Exquisa	●	●					
Jersey Royal	●	●			●		
La Ratte	●	●			●		
Maris Bard	●						
Maris Peer	●					●	
Nicola	●	●			●		
Pentland Javelin	●						●
Pink Fir Apple	●				●		
Roseval	●	●					
Spunta	●					●	

[top to bottom] Truffle, Charlotte, Francine, Shetland Black

BUYING AND STORING potatoes

When choosing potatoes, always look for firm, fresh specimens with a smooth, unblemished skin. Avoid any that are soft and rubbery, that have green or mouldy patches, holes or sprouting eyes. Green patches are caused by exposure to light and indicate that the potato contains an abnormally high level of solanine – a poisonous substance that is not destroyed by cooking. If you discover green patches when peeling your potatoes, the only thing to do is chuck them out.

I generally prefer to purchase my potatoes loose from a greengrocer. Pre-washed potatoes are more likely to spoil quickly than unwashed ones, especially when wrapped in plastic. So although the plastic bags of washed potatoes sold by supermarkets seem convenient, they are really only worth buying if you plan to use them within a couple of days. They are also more expensive than loose potatoes. When buying unwashed potatoes, make sure the soil on them is fresh; if it is slimy or smells unpleasant, the potatoes will not be in good condition.

Organic potatoes are readily available now, and are free of the pesticide residues often detected in the skins of conventionally farmed potatoes – making them a better option if you prefer not to peel them. They almost always taste better, too. Conventionally produced varieties have water and nitrogen added, which gives farmers a bigger yield but dilutes the flavour.

New potatoes don't keep for more than a few days. Maincrop varieties, however, can be kept for up to six months if stored correctly. This means in a cool, dark, well-ventilated place, ideally at about 7°C (45°F). Below this temperature – for example, in the fridge – the starch will convert to sugar, which spoils the flavour. If you purchase potatoes in a plastic bag, transfer them to a brown paper bag before storing – they will become damp in plastic, causing them to rot.

Surprisingly, potatoes tend to bruise quite easily, so always handle them with care. Bruises will turn black when cooked.

To preserve the nutrients, potatoes should be peeled just before you cook them. However, if you do occasionally need to peel them a few hours in advance, keep them in cold water with a little salt and a slice of white bread to prevent discoloration.

ABOUT THE RECIPES...

- Please note that all recipes serve 4 unless otherwise stated.
- All quantities are given in both metric and imperial measures. Do not alternate between the two as they are not interchangable, and doing so might jeopardise the result.
- Medium-size eggs and fresh herbs are used unless otherwise stated.

**[Top to bottom] Maris Piper,
King Edward, La Ratte,
French Charlotte**

tools of the trade

Although you don't have to buy any special equipment for cooking potatoes, here are a few items I find invaluable. Using them correctly not only gets the job done properly but also saves you time. Always buy the best-quality equipment you can afford.

[Top to bottom] French Roseval, Spunta, Red Duke of York, Shetland Black

Deep fryer

You can, of course, deep-fry potatoes in an ordinary saucepan but deep fryers are safer and cleaner to use. The heat is thermostatically controlled and you can close the lid while the potatoes are frying.

Frying pans

Use these for potato sautés, omelettes and pancakes. Heavy-duty frying pans, such as cast iron, are best, since they maintain a steady heat level and the food is less likely to burn. Frying pans with ovenproof handles allow you to transfer food from the hob to the oven to finish cooking.

Grater

You will need a grater for making rösti, boxty and many other traditional potato dishes that call for grated potatoes. Box graters are easy to use. Alternatively you could use the grating disc on a food processor.

Gratin dishes

These shallow baking dishes have low sides so the food can brown easily in the oven and a large surface area so you can enjoy the maximum amount of crisp crust. The best ones can be used over direct heat, to enable you to start the cooking off on the hob before transferring the dish to the oven.

Knives

Good sharp knives are essential for many kitchen tasks. A large, sturdy cook's knife is best for chopping or slicing potatoes. Sharpen the blade regularly on a steel rod – at least once a week to keep it in prime condition.

Mandolin

A good-quality mandolin with an adjustable blade is an expensive piece of equipment but it is a very efficient way of cutting neat potato slices, as thinly as you like. It can also be used for cutting chips and matchstick potatoes, and for shredding.

Potato masher

This is the cheapest way of making mash, although the results won't be quite as smooth as with a potato ricer.

Potato peeler

There are many varieties available but it's best to buy a thin-bladed one. The swivel variety is very good, and also comes in handy for shaving Parmesan cheese. U-shaped peelers, with the blade going straight across the U, can be used with equal ease by right- and left-handers.

Potato ricer or sieve

A potato ricer produces perfect fluffy mashed potato without any lumps at all. A sieve does a pretty good job too, but you will have to push the potato through with a wooden spoon. Buy the largest potato ricer you can find, so you can process the potatoes more speedily.

Don't be tempted to mash potatoes by puréeing them in a food processor, as they will become gluey. Sweet potatoes can be puréed successfully in this way, though.

Roasting tins

Heavy-duty stainless steel or aluminium roasting tins won't buckle in the heat of the oven and can also be used on the hob.

what could be more satisfying than

a potato soup? Nutritious, warming and comforting, it can cost next to nothing to prepare (the White Bean and Potato Soup on page 19, for example) or combine the earthy with the extravagant – like my Chilled Potato and Watercress Soup with Caviar Chantilly (page 19). Potato salads, too, vary from the humble to the luxurious. They are staples of cuisines all over the world, whether you choose a spicy Aloo Chat from India (page 42), a Provençal-inspired Grilled Potato and Fennel Niçoise (page 41) or a Moroccan Sweet Potato and Coriander Salad (page 33). Indeed, for potato salads almost anything goes – the one firm rule is to use waxy rather than floury potatoes so they keep their shape.

Potatoes might not seem an obvious choice for a starter but they don't have to be heavy or filling. It's a question of using them judiciously and combining them with vibrantly flavoured ingredients. Potato Fettunta with Gorgonzola Spread and Crumbled Bacon (page 27) make a simple and elegant canapé, while in the Peruvian dish, Causa (page 23), a fiery salsa adds interest to layered purple and saffron potatoes.

SOUPS,
STARTERS
AND SALADS

potato, smoked bacon and nettle soup

Heat 50g (2oz) of the butter in a heavy-based pan, add the onion and leek and sweat for 8–10 minutes, until soft. Add the potatoes and cook for 5 minutes. Pour in the stock and bring to the boil, then reduce the heat and simmer for 25–30 minutes. Meanwhile, blanch the nettles in a large pan of boiling water, drain well and squeeze out the excess water.

Remove half the soup from the pan and blitz to a purée in a blender. Pour it into a clean pan, add the cream, nettles, the remaining soup, nutmeg and some seasoning and bring to the boil. Meanwhile, heat the remaining butter in a pan, add the bacon and diced bread and cook until golden. Pour the soup into bowls, sprinkle over the bacon and croûtons and serve.

75g (3oz) unsalted butter

1 onion, diced

1 leek, thinly sliced

600g (1lb 5oz) waxy potatoes, peeled and cut into 1cm ($^{1}/_{2}$ in) cubes

750ml (1$^{1}/_{4}$ pints) well-flavoured chicken stock

100g (4oz) nettles

300ml ($^{1}/_{2}$ pint) single cream

Freshly grated nutmeg

75g (3oz) smoked bacon, cut into small dice

2 slices of white bread, crusts removed, cut into 1cm ($^{1}/_{2}$ in) dice

Salt and freshly ground black pepper

tattie hushie (potato, cauliflower and oatmeal soup)

A rich, comforting soup from Lancashire – not Scotland, as the name might suggest.

Heat the butter in a pan, add the leek and cauliflower and cook gently for a few minutes. Add the potatoes, then cover and sweat for 10 minutes. Mix together the milk and oatmeal and pour them over the vegetables. Add the stock, bring to the boil and simmer until the vegetables are tender. Blitz the soup to a purée in a blender, then reheat gently and season to taste.

25g (1oz) unsalted butter

1 leek, sliced

200g (7oz) cauliflower, cut into small florets

550g (1$^{1}/_{4}$ lb) floury potatoes, peeled and diced

600ml (1 pint) full-fat milk

50g (2oz) coarse oatmeal

600ml (1 pint) well-flavoured chicken stock

Salt and freshly ground black pepper

sweet potato, fourme d'ambert and chipotle chilli soup

This lovely soup showcases this delicate vegetable at its best, with a combination of sweet, spicy and savoury flavours.

Cut the chillies in half lengthways and shake out the seeds. Place the chillies in a bowl, cover with boiling water and leave to soak for 30 minutes, then drain and chop. Heat the butter in a pan, add the onion, carrot, celery and sage and cook over a low heat for 4–5 minutes, until softened. Add the sweet potatoes, potatoes and chillies, cover and sweat for 5 minutes. Pour in the chicken stock and bring to the boil, then reduce the heat and simmer for 40–45 minutes, until the vegetables are falling apart. Pour the soup into a blender and blitz until smooth and velvety. Return to the heat and season with nutmeg, salt and pepper.

Put the cheese and cream in a small pan and heat gently, stirring, until smooth. Pour the soup into serving bowls, pour the cheese cream over the top and blend in lightly. Scatter over the coriander and serve.

2 chipotle chillies

25g (1oz) unsalted butter

1 onion, chopped

1 carrot, chopped

1 celery stick, chopped

2 sage leaves, chopped

450g (1lb) sweet potatoes, peeled and chopped

200g (7oz) potatoes, peeled and chopped

1 litre (1³/₄ pints) well-flavoured chicken stock

Freshly grated nutmeg

75g (3oz) Fourme d'Ambert cheese (or other mild blue cheese)

100ml (3¹/₂ fl oz) double cream

2 tablespoons chopped coriander

Salt and freshly ground black pepper

cuLLen skiNk (smoked haddock and potato soup)

Cullen skink can be made in various ways and I've probably tried them all in my time. It varies from a broth to a thickened soup, like my recipe below. When I think of smoked haddock I always think of soft poached eggs as an accompaniment, so I decided to add them to this traditional Scottish soup and discovered a real winner.

Put the smoked haddock in a saucepan, pour over the hot milk and add half the onion and the mace. Bring just to the boil, then add the water. Bring back to the boil and simmer for 4–5 minutes, until the fish is cooked. Remove from the heat, take out the fish with a slotted spoon and place in a bowl to cool. Strain the cooking liquid and set aside. Flake the fish, removing the skin and bones.

Melt the butter in a large pan, add the remaining onion and cook until soft. Add the potatoes and sweat for 5 minutes. Pour over the reserved cooking liquid and simmer until the potatoes are tender. Pour into a blender and blitz to a purée, then pour into a clean pan. Season with nutmeg, salt and pepper, stir in the flaked fish and keep warm.
Poach the eggs in the classic manner (see page 104), then remove from the pan and drain well. Pour the soup into soup bowls, place a poached egg in the centre of each portion and sprinkle over the parsley.

---

tip

ALWAYS BUY NATURAL SMOKED HADDOCK, not the lurid, bright-yellow dyed version available from some fishmongers, who are concerned more with appearance than with taste.

450g (1lb) natural smoked haddock, on the bone

600ml (1 pint) hot full-fat milk

2 onions, sliced

1 blade of mace

600ml (1 pint) water

75g (3oz) unsalted butter

4 medium-sized floury potatoes, peeled and diced

Freshly grated nutmeg

4 eggs

2 tablespoons chopped parsley

Salt and freshly ground black pepper

Chilled potato and watercress soup with caviar chantilly

chilled potato and watercress soup with caviar chantilly

Pick the leaves from one bunch of watercress and set aside. Blanch the other bunch and the stalks in boiling water, then drain, refresh in cold water and drain again. Chop finely.

Heat the butter in a pan, add the onion, leeks and potatoes, then cover and sweat over a low heat until softened. Pour in the chicken stock, add the chopped watercress and bring to the boil. Simmer for 20–25 minutes, until the potatoes are falling apart. Pour the soup into a blender and blitz to a purée. Leave to cool, then stir in the double cream. Season to taste and chill thoroughly.

Pour into serving bowls, garnish with the reserved watercress leaves, then place a dollop of cream in the centre of each portion and top it with the caviar.

2 bunches of watercress

50g (2oz) unsalted butter

1 onion, chopped

2 leeks, white part only, chopped

450g (1lb) floury potatoes, peeled and diced

900ml (1 1/2 pints) chicken stock

120ml (4fl oz) double cream

Salt and freshly ground black pepper

For the caviar chantilly:

100ml (3 1/2 fl oz) double cream, semi-whipped

20g (3/4 oz) caviar

fagioli bianchi et patata (white bean and potato soup)

Drain the beans, place them in a large pan and cover with fresh water. Add the herbs and bring to the boil, then simmer for 1 hour. Add the potatoes and garlic and simmer gently for a further 30 minutes, until the beans and potatoes are soft. Pour into a blender and blitz to a smooth purée, then return to the pan, season to taste and keep warm. If the soup is too thick, thin it with a little water.

Heat half the oil in a frying pan, add the cubes of bread and fry until golden. Drain on kitchen paper and sprinkle with the paprika. Pour the soup into serving bowls, sprinkle with the paprika croûtons, drizzle over the remaining olive oil and serve.

250g (9oz) dried cannellini beans, soaked in cold water overnight

6 sage leaves

A sprig of rosemary

250g (9oz) floury potatoes, peeled and cut into small dice

4 garlic cloves, crushed

6 tablespoons virgin olive oil

2 slices of thick country bread, cut into 1cm (1/2 in) cubes

1 teaspoon paprika

Salt and freshly ground black pepper

roasted sweet potato bisque with avocado and lime salsa

Preheat the oven to 200°C/400°F/gas mark 6. Place the sweet potatoes in a baking tin, pour over 4 tablespoons of the olive oil and roast for 40 minutes or until tender – don't let them brown too much, though.

Heat the remaining oil in a large pan, add the onion, garlic and grated ginger and cook gently for 5 minutes. Add the roasted sweet potatoes, red chilli, cinnamon and some seasoning, then pour in the stock and bring to the boil. Reduce the heat and simmer for 15 minutes. Pour the soup into a blender and blitz to a smooth purée, then pour it into a large bowl. Stir in the double cream, maple syrup and lime juice and chill thoroughly.

For the salsa, put the avocado cubes in a bowl, add all the remaining ingredients and mix well. Season to taste.

To serve, pour the soup into chilled soup bowls and place a spoonful of avocado and lime salsa in the centre of each one.

650g (1lb 6oz) sweet potatoes, peeled and cut into large chunks

6 tablespoons olive oil

1 onion, finely chopped

1 garlic clove, crushed

5cm (2in) piece of fresh root ginger, grated

1 small red chilli, deseeded and thinly sliced

1/2 teaspoon ground cinnamon

750ml (1 1/4 pints) good vegetable or chicken stock

120ml (4fl oz) double cream

2 tablespoons maple syrup

Juice of 2 limes

Salt and freshly ground black pepper

For the salsa:

1 avocado, peeled, stoned and cut into small cubes

2 plum tomatoes, skinned, deseeded and chopped

4 tablespoons lime juice

2 spring onions, chopped

1 small red chilli, deseeded and chopped

1 tablespoon roughly chopped coriander

3 tablespoons olive oil

potage parmentier (potato and Leek soup)

A well-made soup is both inexpensive and satisfying, and can be served as a starter, a light meal or a main dish. This soup is easy to prepare and forms a base for many different variations (see below). Served chilled, it becomes the classic Vichyssoise.

Heat the butter in a pan, add the onion and leeks, then cover and sweat until tender but not coloured. Pour in the stock and bring to the boil. Add the potatoes and simmer for 25–30 minutes, until tender. Pour the soup into a blender and blitz to a very smooth purée. Return to the pan, reheat gently and stir in the cream and some seasoning. Serve immediately, sprinkled with the chives.

25g (1oz) unsalted butter

1/2 onion, sliced

2 large leeks, white part only, sliced

1 litre (1³/4 pints) well-flavoured chicken stock

350g (12oz) floury potatoes, peeled and chopped

120ml (4fl oz) double cream

1 tablespoon chopped chives

Salt and freshly ground black pepper

variations

- *Stir in 75g (3oz) finely chopped herbs with the cream and serve chilled. Tarragon, chervil and parsley are good.*
- *Add 200g (7oz) blanched spinach with the onion and leeks.*
- *Replace the leeks with celery.*

causa

*This chilled potato dish from Peru is made differently in every village and
town. I particularly like the way it is moulded and layered to show off the
contrasting colours.*

Serves 6–8

Cook the truffle potatoes in a pan of boiling salted water until tender.
Drain and leave until cool enough to handle, then peel. Peel the new
potatoes and put them in a separate pan with the saffron. Cover with
boiling salted water and simmer until tender, then drain well. Mash the
truffle potatoes and new potatoes separately, or pass them through a
sieve, to give a smooth purée. Beat half the butter into each purée,
followed by half the olive oil and season to taste. Mix the tuna with the
mayonnaise and season to taste.

Take 6–8 metal rings, about 10cm (4in) in diameter, and grease the
insides with oil. Place a thin layer of truffle potato purée in each one,
followed by some of the tuna mixture, then a layer of saffron potato
purée, then more tuna. Top with truffle potato again, then tuna, and
finish with saffron potatoes. Smooth the tops with a palette knife and
chill for 2–3 hours, until firm. Meanwhile, mix all the dressing
ingredients together, season to taste and leave to infuse for 1 hour.

To serve, carefully unmould the potato causa onto serving plates and
pour the dressing over and around each one.

350g (12oz) truffle potatoes (black
   potatoes)
350g (12oz) new potatoes
A good pinch of saffron strands
75g (3oz) unsalted butter
6 tablespoons olive oil
175g (6oz) canned tuna in olive oil, drained
4 tablespoons good-quality mayonnaise
Salt and freshly ground black pepper

For the dressing:
2 tablespoons vegetable oil
1 garlic clove, crushed
4 spring onions, finely chopped
1 habanero chilli, deseeded and finely
   chopped
2 plum tomatoes, cut into 5mm (1/4 in) dice
2 anchovy fillets, finely chopped
Juice and finely grated zest of 1 lime
1 tablespoon chopped coriander
1 tablespoon honey
1 teaspoon baby capers, rinsed and drained
A pinch of ground cumin

GRILLED SQUID WITH CHILLI-PICKLED POTATOES AND SHALLOTS

Cut the unpeeled potatoes into slices 1cm ($^1/_2$ in) thick and place on a tray. Sprinkle with the coarse salt and leave for 1 hour to help extract the liquid. Wash off the salt and dry the potatoes in a cloth. Bring a pan of water to the boil, add the potatoes and cook for 5 minutes, then drain well.

Put the vinegar, sugar and chilli flakes in a pan and bring slowly to the boil. Pour into a bowl and leave to cool, then add the potatoes, shallots, garlic, herbs and 4 tablespoons of the olive oil. Season and leave to marinate for 30 minutes at room temperature.

Cut each cleaned squid body open to make a flat piece. Using a sharp knife, score the inner side with parallel criss-cross lines about 1cm ($^1/_2$ in) apart.

Toss the squid with the remaining olive oil, season and place scored-side down on a hot ridged grill pan or a barbecue. Cook for 1–2 minutes, then turn and briefly cook the other side. Add to the pickled potatoes while hot and leave for a further 30 minutes to allow the flavours to develop. Serve at room temperature with lots of crusty bread.

250g (9oz) salad potatoes

1 tablespoon coarse salt

150ml ($^1/_4$ pint) white wine vinegar

3 tablespoons caster sugar

$^1/_2$ teaspoon dried red chilli flakes

2 small shallots, sliced into rings

1 garlic clove, crushed

1 teaspoon chopped mint

1 tablespoon chopped coriander

6 tablespoons olive oil

450g (1lb) baby squid, cleaned, tentacles reserved

Salt and freshly ground black pepper

patatas tatas

Recently some fellow chefs and I visited Barcelona on a gastronomic tour of the city's famed restaurants. Being typical chefs, we found time between meals to experience some of Spain's legendary tapas bars, serving simple, tasty hors d'oeuvres. Here's a recipe I picked up at one of them.

Cook the potatoes in their skins in boiling salted water until just tender, then drain and cool slightly before peeling them (or leave the skins on if you prefer). Cut into thick slices and set aside.

Heat the butter in a pan, add the onion, garlic and smoked paprika and cook gently until softened. Add the tomatoes and cook for 2–3 minutes, until they begin to soften, then season with salt and pepper. Pour in the cream and bring to the boil. Simmer for 2 minutes, then remove from the heat, add the cheese and stir it in to form a sauce. Place the potatoes in a serving dish, pour over the cheese and tomato sauce and serve.

1kg (2^1/4 lb) waxy new potatoes

25g (1oz) unsalted butter

1 onion, finely chopped

1 garlic clove, crushed

^{1}/2 teaspoon smoked paprika

4 plum tomatoes, skinned, deseeded and roughly chopped into large pieces

150ml (^{1}/4 pint) double cream

150g (5oz) Manchego cheese, grated

Salt and freshly ground black pepper

cypriot hot potatoes with cracked coriander seeds

Technically not a salad, you may say, but I like to serve it as one. It is full of enticing flavours and aromas, especially when you lift the lid from the pan – try it and you'll see what I mean.

Preheat the oven to 200°C/400°F/gas mark 6. Heat the olive oil in a flameproof casserole, add the potatoes and fry until golden all over. Season lightly, then cover, transfer to the oven and cook for 15–20 minutes, until just tender. Remove the casserole from the oven and place over a medium heat. Pour over the wine and scatter over the cracked coriander seeds, then cover with a tight-fitting lid and leave to steam for 5–8 minutes, until all the liquid has evaporated. Remove the lid, season to taste and serve.

4 tablespoons olive oil

450g (1lb) new potatoes (Cyprus or Jersey Royals), halved but not peeled

120ml (4fl oz) dry white wine

2 tablespoons coriander seeds, lightly cracked

Salt and freshly ground black pepper

potato fettunta with gorgonzola spread and crumbled bacon

Fettunta are very similar to crostini or bruschetta – crisp bread croûtes topped with all manner of ingredients. Here, baked potato slices replace the bread. They make an ideal canapé, appetiser or titbit.

Preheat the oven to 200°C/400°F/gas mark 6. Cut each potato lengthways into slices 1cm ($^1/_2$ in) thick (don't peel them) and parboil in salted water for 2–3 minutes. Drain well and dry. Place the potato slices on a baking sheet, brush on both sides with the olive oil and season with salt and pepper. Bake for 15–20 minutes, until golden.

Meanwhile, grill the bacon rashers until very crisp, then break them up into large pieces and set aside. Put the spring onions and gorgonzola in a bowl and crush lightly with a fork to break the cheese down slightly. Stir in the walnut oil and season to taste.

Top the warm potato slices with a good dollop of the gorgonzola mixture. Put the bacon on top and serve.

5 small baking potatoes

4 tablespoons olive oil

10 streaky bacon rashers, rind removed

2 spring onions, shredded

125g (4$^1/_2$ oz) gorgonzola cheese

1 tablespoon walnut oil

Salt and freshly ground black pepper

truffle potato-stuffed quesadillas with crab and chorizo

This makes a great lunchtime dish or an unusual starter when you're looking for something a little different.

Boil the truffle potatoes in their skins until tender, then drain well. Peel them and dice roughly. Heat the butter in a pan, add the onion, chilli and garlic and sweat until softened but not coloured. Add the diced potatoes and cook for 12 minutes. Remove from the heat, crush the potatoes coarsely with a fork and stir in half the cream cheese to bind. Season to taste.

Mix the crab meat with the coriander, the grated cheese, the diced chorizo and the remaining cream cheese and season to taste. Lay out 4 of the tortillas on a flat surface, spread the potato mixture over them and cover with the crab mixture. Place the remaining tortillas on top and press down lightly. Grill the stuffed quesadillas on a ridged grill pan (or sauté them in a little extra butter in a frying pan) until charred and golden, turning them once during cooking.

To serve, cut the quesadillas into wedges and garnish with sprigs of fresh coriander. I also like to serve them topped with a dollop of soured cream, grated cheese and a little hot salsa.

300g (11oz) truffle potatoes (black potatoes)

25g (1oz) unsalted butter

1 onion, finely chopped

1 green chilli, deseeded and finely chopped

2 garlic cloves, crushed

6 tablespoons cream cheese

250g (9oz) fresh white crab meat

2 tablespoons chopped coriander

50g (2oz) mature Cheddar or Monterey Jack cheese, grated

75g (3oz) chorizo, skinned and cut into 5mm (1/4 in) dice

8 x 15cm (6in) flour tortillas

Salt and freshly ground black pepper

Soured cream, more grated cheese and your favourite hot salsa, to serve

Baby Beet, Potato and Blue Cheese Salad

Roasting beetroot in a sweet and sour dressing gives it a wonderful flavour.

Preheat the oven to 200°C/400°F/gas mark 6. Trim the beetroots and wash them well. Place in a roasting tin, drizzle with the olive oil and red wine vinegar, then sprinkle with the brown sugar. Roast in the oven for 40–45 minutes, until tender.

Cook the potatoes in their skins in boiling salted water until tender, then drain well and cut in half. Put them in a bowl with the cooked beetroot and scatter the cheese on top. Drizzle over the walnut oil, scatter over the walnuts, then season with coarse salt and cracked black pepper.

6 baby beetroots, whole or cut in half, depending on size
3 tablespoons olive oil
1 tablespoon good-quality red wine vinegar
1 heaped teaspoon brown sugar
450g (1lb) baby Jersey Royal potatoes
175g (6oz) Stilton or gorgonzola cheese, roughly chopped
3 tablespoons walnut oil
3 tablespoons walnut halves, toasted and roughly chopped
Coarse salt and freshly cracked black pepper

Patatosalata (Cretan Potato Salad)

Tasty and colourful, this makes ideal summer fare, a reminder of one of the world's loveliest destinations.

Cook the potatoes in their skins in boiling salted water until just tender, then drain and leave until cool enough to handle. Peel the potatoes and place in a bowl.

Make a dressing by whisking together the red wine vinegar, mustard and olive oil. Pour it over the potatoes while they are still warm. Mix in the remaining ingredients and leave to marinate for at least 3 hours before serving.

50g (1lb) salad potatoes
1 tablespoon red wine vinegar
1/2 teaspoon Dijon mustard
5 tablespoons olive oil
150g (5oz) feta or kefalotiri cheese, crumbled into large pieces
1 tablespoon chopped mint
1 teaspoon chopped oregano
1 red onion, thinly sliced
3 spring onions, chopped
16 black olives
1 tablespoon finely chopped preserved lemon
Salt and freshly ground black pepper

TIP

PRESERVED SALTED LEMONS are one of the definitive flavours of Moroccan cooking, used in all manner of dishes, from tagines to salads. You can buy them from some delicatessens and large supermarkets.

Baby beet, potato and blue cheese salad

warm potato and shellfish salad

This warm shellfish salad is of Spanish origin. The saffron dressing complements the seafood beautifully, vibrant in colour and taste.

Heat the olive oil in a large deep pan, add the onion, tomatoes, roasted red pepper and garlic and cook over a medium heat for 1–2 minutes. Raise the heat to high, add the squid and cook for 2 minutes, then add the potatoes, fish stock and sherry and leave to cook gently for 20 minutes. Add the clams, mussels and king prawns, cover and cook gently for a further 2–3 minutes. Using a slotted spoon, transfer all the ingredients to a large plate. Strain the juices left in the pan and set aside.

For the dressing, crush the garlic with the saffron in a mortar. Add the basil and parsley and crush to a paste, then mix in the lemon juice, olive oil and the reserved cooking juices. Adjust the seasoning to taste and drizzle the dressing over the shellfish. Serve warm, with lots of crusty bread.

tip

TO CLEAN MUSSELS AND CLAMS, scrub them well under cold running water and discard any open ones that don't close when tapped on the work surface. With mussels, you will also need to pull out and discard the 'beard'.

2 tablespoons olive oil

1 onion, finely chopped

3 plum tomatoes, skinned, deseeded and chopped

1 red pepper, roasted, skinned, deseeded and diced

1 garlic clove, crushed

8 small squid, cleaned and cut into rings

450g (1lb) small salad potatoes, peeled and diced

100ml (3^1/2 fl oz) fish stock

4 tablespoons dry sherry

350g (12oz) clams, cleaned (see Tip)

350g (12oz) mussels, cleaned (see Tip)

20 raw king prawns, peeled and de-veined (see Tip on page 139)

For the dressing:

2 garlic cloves, chopped

A good pinch of saffron strands

10 basil leaves

4 tablespoons chopped flat-leaf parsley

Juice of 1 lemon

100ml (3^1/2 fl oz) olive oil

Salt and freshly ground black pepper

moroccan sweet potato and coriander salad

Morocco boasts one of the most exciting cuisines in the world, a subtle blend of African and European influences. On a recent family holiday in Marrakech, I experienced typical street food at the Djema'a al Fna, the world-renowned square where thousands of people gather nightly to enjoy good food and a lively atmosphere. Here's a salad I have adapted from one prepared by a vendor in the square.

Heat 100ml (3^{1}/$_{2}$ fl oz) of the olive oil in a large pan, add the onions, ginger and chillies and sauté until tender but not coloured. Add the sweet potatoes, saffron, cumin seeds, lemon juice and smoked paprika, then pour in enough water just to cover. Cover the pan with a lid, reduce the heat and cook for 10–12 minutes, until the potatoes are just tender. Stir in the coriander, mint and preserved lemon, then pour over the remaining oil and adjust the seasoning. Transfer to a bowl and leave to cool before serving.

150ml (^{1}/$_{4}$ pint) good-quality olive oil

2 onions, thinly sliced

1cm (^{1}/$_{2}$ in) piece of fresh root ginger, finely chopped

2 red chillies, deseeded and thinly sliced

600g (1lb 5oz) small, white-fleshed sweet potatoes, peeled and cut into slices 3mm (^{1}/$_{8}$ in) thick

A pinch of saffron strands

^{1}/$_{2}$ teaspoon cumin seeds, toasted briefly in a dry frying pan

Juice of 1 lemon

^{1}/$_{2}$ teaspoon smoked paprika

3 tablespoons chopped coriander

1 tablespoon chopped mint

1 tablespoon finely chopped preserved lemon (see Tip on page 30)

Salt and freshly ground black pepper

Roast potato salad with smoked salmon

Roast potato salad with smoked salmon

I have always liked the combination of smoked fish and potatoes. Here, Jersey Royals and a piquant dressing act as the perfect foil for the salmon.

Preheat the oven to 190°C/375°F/gas mark 5. Wash the potatoes, then put them in a roasting tin, toss with 60ml (2fl oz) of the olive oil, and season with salt. Roast for about 40 minutes, until golden and tender, then remove from the oven and leave to cool slightly.

Whisk the vinegar and the remaining olive oil together to make a dressing and season to taste. Cut the potatoes in half and place in a bowl with the spring onions, capers, gherkins and chopped eggs. Pour over the dressing and adjust the seasoning.

Spread the smoked salmon out on 4 serving plates and arrange the potato salad on top. If you're a salmon lover like me, place a little extra salmon on top, too. Sprinkle with the tarragon and serve.

350g (12oz) small Jersey Royal potatoes

150ml (¼ pint) olive oil

2 tablespoons sherry vinegar

2 spring onions, cut into slices 3mm (⅛ in) thick

1 tablespoon superfine capers, drained

6 small cocktail gherkins, thinly sliced

2 eggs, hard-boiled and finely chopped

300g (11oz) thinly sliced smoked salmon

1 teaspoon chopped tarragon

Salt and freshly ground black pepper

Tricolour potato salad

This simple potato salad looks stunning, using three varieties of potatoes that work so well together visually.

Cut the unpeeled potatoes into slices 5mm (¼ in) thick, preferably on a mandolin. Cook them separately in pans of boiling salted water for 4–5 minutes, until just tender, then remove with a slotted spoon and place in a bowl.

Make the dressing by whisking the mustard with the vinegar, garlic and a little salt, then whisking in the oil. Add the herbs, then toss the dressing with the hot potato slices. Adjust the seasoning and serve warm.

200g (7oz) truffle potatoes (black potatoes)

200g (7oz) red-skinned potatoes

200g (7oz) new potatoes

Salt and freshly ground black pepper

For the dressing:

1 teaspoon Dijon mustard

1 tablespoon red wine vinegar

1 garlic clove, crushed

3 tablespoons virgin olive oil

2 tablespoons each chopped mint and chives

salad monégasque with chargrilled sardines

Salad monégasque is similar to salade niçoise and is prepared daily in cafés and brasseries throughout France. It is normally served on its own but I prefer it with chargrilled fish. Mackerel would work just as well as sardines.

Cook the unpeeled potatoes and the French beans in separate pans of boiling salted water until just tender, then drain well. For the dressing, whisk the vinegar, garlic, mustard and a little salt together in a large bowl, then whisk in the oil. Add the potatoes and beans to the bowl, then add all the remaining ingredients except the sardines. Toss gently and season with salt and pepper.

Heat a ridged grill pan and brush with a little oil. Place the sardine fillets on the grill and cook for 2–3 minutes on each side, until golden. Arrange the salad on serving plates, top with the chargrilled sardines and drizzle over a little of the dressing left in the bowl.

225g (8oz) small new potatoes

150g (5oz) French beans

4 anchovy fillets, cut into strips

2 teaspoons superfine capers, rinsed and drained

4 radishes, thinly shaved

12 black olives, pitted

1 celery stick, thinly sliced

12 cherry tomatoes, halved

2 hard-boiled eggs, cut into quarters

4 x 225g (8oz) fresh sardines, filleted

Salt and freshly ground black pepper

For the dressing:

2 tablespoons good-quality white wine vinegar

2 garlic cloves, crushed

1 teaspoon Dijon mustard

6 tablespoons olive oil, plus extra for grilling

salt-baked potato salad

This is an adaptation of an idea by Todd English, renowned chef of Olives Restaurant in Boston. I love the simple idea of filling a jacket potato with a salad – I've used a variation of Waldorf salad here, which works wonderfully well with the hot baked potato.

Bake the potatoes until tender (see page 70), then slice a lid off the top of each one. Scoop out a little of the centre with a spoon and discard. Combine the salad leaves, apples, walnuts, celery and ham in a salad bowl.

Make the dressing by whisking together the mustard, tarragon, shallots, and vinegar, then gradually whisking in the olive oil until emulsified. Add the vinaigrette to the salad bowl, season and toss well. Arrange the salad on top of the potatoes, sprinkle over the crumbled Roquefort and serve immediately.

4 large floury potatoes

¹/2 chicory head, cut into strips

25g (1oz) rocket

2 Granny Smith apples, cored and chopped

2 tablespoons chopped walnuts

1 celery stick, sliced

75g (3oz) cooked ham, cut into strips

75g (3oz) Roquefort cheese, crumbled

Salt and freshly ground black pepper

For the dressing:

1 teaspoon Dijon mustard

1 tablespoon chopped tarragon

2 shallots, finely chopped

1 tablespoon cider vinegar

4 tablespoons olive oil

saffron potato, pear and fennel salad

Sliced raw fennel has a wonderful aroma and adds a good crunch to potato salads. Serve with grilled fish for a light lunch.

Cook the potatoes in their skins in boiling salted water until just tender, then drain well and leave until cool enough to handle. Peel the potatoes, cut them into slices 5mm (¹/4 in) thick and place in a large bowl.

Whisk together all the ingredients for the dressing, pour it over the potatoes and toss well. Season to taste and leave for about 30 minutes.

Slice the fennel very thinly, preferably on a mandolin (reserve the fronds for garnish), and add to the potatoes. Peel, core and thinly slice the pear, add to the potatoes and toss. Adjust the seasoning, garnish and serve.

350g (12oz) waxy potatoes, preferably La Ratte or Charlotte

2 fennel bulbs

1 large, ripe Conference pear

For the dressing:

4 tablespoons olive oil

2 tablespoons walnut oil

1 tablespoon sherry vinegar

A good pinch of saffron strands

2 tablespoons honey

Salt and freshly ground black pepper

smoked duck, potato and cep salad

This elegant salad makes a wonderful starter for a dinner party. Smoked chicken works as well as duck, and is easily available and less expensive.

Cook the potatoes in their skins in boiling salted water until just tender, then drain well. Cut them into slices 1cm (¹/2 in) thick, then fry in the olive oil for 3–4 minutes on each side, until golden. Add the sliced ceps and the walnuts and sauté for a minute longer. Season to taste, remove from the heat and keep warm.

For the dressing, combine the shallot, mustard, sherry vinegar, garlic and herbs in a small bowl, then whisk in both oils and season with salt and pepper. Place the salad leaves in a bowl, toss with a little of the dressing and adjust the seasoning. Arrange the salad leaves on 4 serving plates and top with the slices of smoked duck. Scatter the potato mixture on top and drizzle over the remaining dressing, then serve immediately.

150g (5oz) new potatoes

4 tablespoons olive oil

4 large fresh cep (porcini) mushrooms (or chestnut mushrooms), sliced

24 walnut halves

150g (5oz) mixed salad leaves

2 smoked duck breasts, thinly sliced

Salt and freshly ground black pepper

For the dressing:

1 shallot, finely chopped

¹/2 teaspoon Dijon mustard

2 tablespoons sherry vinegar

1 garlic clove, crushed

1 tablespoon chopped flat-leaf parsley

1 tablespoon chopped tarragon

4 tablespoons olive oil

2 tablespoons walnut oil

GRILLED potato AND fenneL Niçoise

A simple but tasty salad, full of the robust flavours of Provence. Don't worry if you haven't got a pestle and mortar for the dressing; use a small blender instead.

Remove any fronds from the fennel and set aside. Peel the fennel with a potato peeler to remove the fibrous outer layer. Cut each bulb in half lengthways, then cut each half into eighths. Trim off a little of the root from each piece but be careful to leave the layers attached at the root end.

Bring 2 pans of water to the boil. Add the fennel to one and the new potatoes to the other. Cook the fennel for 3–4 minutes, then drain in a colander. Let the new potatoes cook on until they are just tender when pierced with a knife. Drain in a colander and cool slightly before cutting them in half lengthways. Heat a ridged grill pan, toss the fennel wedges and potatoes in the olive oil and season with salt and pepper. Cook on the grill, turning them often, until golden and tender.

Meanwhile, prepare the dressing. Place the garlic, basil and a good pinch of salt in a mortar and crush to a paste. Stir in the remaining ingredients and season to taste.

Put the grilled potatoes and fennel in a bowl, pour over the dressing and garnish with any reserved fennel fronds.

3 fennel bulbs

350g (12oz) large new potatoes

4 tablespoons olive oil

Salt and freshly ground black pepper

For the dressing:

1 garlic clove, chopped

8 basil leaves

2 red peppers, roasted, skinned, deseeded
    and finely chopped

10 black olives, pitted and finely chopped

2 shallots, finely chopped

4 anchovy fillets, finely chopped

5 tablespoons olive oil

Juice of $\frac{1}{2}$ lemon

aloo chat

This Indian salad, served at room temperature, is fantastic with a tart apple and grape chutney. It also makes a nice addition to an Asian meal.

Heat the ghee or clarified butter in a frying pan, add the onion and cook over a low heat until translucent. Add the potatoes, chilli, turmeric, ground coriander, cumin seeds and a little salt and fry for 10–15 minutes, until the potatoes are lightly browned.

Add the water and bring to the boil. Reduce the heat to a simmer and cook gently until all the liquid has been absorbed and the potatoes are tender. Leave to cool, then arrange in a serving dish. Scatter over the coconut shavings and coriander leaves before serving.

100g (4oz) ghee or clarified butter (see Tip on page 153)

1 small onion, finely chopped

450g (1lb) small waxy potatoes, peeled and cut lengthways in half

1 small red chilli, deseeded and thinly sliced

1 teaspoon ground turmeric

2 teaspoons ground coriander

1 teaspoon cumin seeds, toasted briefly in a dry frying pan

150ml (¼ pint) water

Flesh from ½ small coconut, cut into shavings (see Tip)

Fresh coriander leaves, to garnish

Salt

tip

TO SHAVE FRESH COCONUT, cut a coconut in half with a saw and pour off the liquid. Knock the base of the coconut hard with a rolling pin to loosen the flesh, then run a knife around the edge – the flesh should come away in one piece. Cut into shavings with a potato peeler or a mandolin.

warm potato salad with ham, shallot and mustard dressing

The ingredients for this salad form the recipe for the classic French dish jambon persillé (jellied ham with parsley). It occurred to me one day to try a potato salad using virtually the same ingredients. It worked well, so here it is.

Cook the potatoes in boiling salted water until tender, then drain and place in a bowl. Add the gammon, shallots, capers, gherkins and parsley and toss together.

For the dressing, put the vinegar and mustard in a bowl, whisk in the olive oil and season to taste. Pour the dressing over the potatoes and toss to blend all the ingredients. Leave for 10–15 minutes to allow the potatoes to absorb the flavours of the dressing. Serve warm.

650g (1lb 6oz) new potatoes, peeled

100g (4oz) cooked gammon, chopped

2 shallots, chopped

2 tablespoons superfine capers, rinsed and drained

8 cocktail gherkins, chopped

3 tablespoons chopped flat-leaf parsley

For the dressing:

1 tablespoon red wine vinegar

1 teaspoon Dijon mustard

4 tablespoons olive oil

Salt and freshly ground black pepper

Aloo chat

mashed potato is the ultimate

comfort food, a rich, creamy, soothing purée that seems eternally associated with childhood. Yet recently it's come of age, as chefs have enriched it with more and more butter, cream and oil and incorporated new flavours. I've done my share of reinventing mash and this chapter contains some of my favourites, such as Charred Onion and Bacon Mash (page 49) and Truffle, Morel and Sweetcorn Mash (page 49). But you'll also find recipes here for basic mash (page 46) and traditional dishes such as the Irish Champ (page 50).

Dumplings might not be as popular as mash but they deserve to be. In northern Europe they are something of an art form – delicate and featherlight, an ideal vehicle for soaking up the rich juices of a soup or stew. Potatoes make some of the lightest dumplings of all, like the little Italian gnocchi (see page 51), which are poached and served with a sauce. Like many potato recipes, they lend themselves to an infinite range of variations: you can vary the basic gnocchi recipe by adding different flavourings or, for a complete change, try Sweet Potato Gnocchi with Red Pepper and Basil (page 52).

mash,
gnocchi and
dumplings

Everyone knows how to make mash but very few people know how to do it properly. For perfect results, follow the tips below:

- Use floury potatoes, such as Desiree or Maris Piper.
- Don't peel the potatoes until just before cooking them, otherwise they will go hard.
- Put the potatoes in a pan of cold water and bring to the boil, rather than putting them straight into boiling water.
- Don't overcook them or they will disintegrate and go mushy.
- Mash them immediately; they will become glutinous if left to stand.
- Work the butter in thoroughly to give a really velvety smoothness.
- Mix in the hot milk gradually; because potatoes vary in starch content, adding too much can make them runny.
- Serve mash immediately; it doesn't reheat well.

perfect mashed potatoes

900g (2lb) even-sized floury potatoes, peeled and cut into chunks
100g (4oz) unsalted butter
About 100ml (3¹/₂ fl oz) hot full-fat milk
4 tablespoons double cream
Salt and freshly ground black pepper

Place the potatoes in a pan, cover with cold water, then add a little salt and bring to the boil. Reduce the heat and simmer until tender. Drain well in a colander and return to the pan. Mash with a potato masher or pass the potatoes through a potato ricer or sieve.

Beat in the butter with a wooden spoon, then gradually mix in the hot milk, followed by the cream, adding just enough to achieve the consistency you prefer. Beat until fluffy and light, then season to taste. The mash should be buttery, creamy and velvety in texture. Now you have the perfect mash!

perfect mashed potatoes

variations on the perfect mashed potato...

parsnip, potato and honey mustard mash

400g (14oz) parsnips, peeled and cut into chunks

250g (9oz) floury potatoes, peeled and cut into chunks

150ml (¼ pint) hot full-fat milk

50g (2oz) unsalted butter

4 tablespoons double cream

1 tablespoon honey

2 tablespoons wholegrain mustard

Salt and freshly ground black pepper

Place the parsnips and potatoes in a pan, cover with cold water, then add a little salt and bring to the boil. Reduce the heat and simmer until almost tender. Drain through a colander and return to the pan.

Pour over the milk and cook for a further 5–8 minutes, until the potatoes are tender.

Remove from the heat, add the butter, cream, honey and mustard and mash with a potato masher until smooth. Season to taste.

mashed potatoes with mascarpone and tomatoes

So simple, so tasty. Try it with fish, such as salmon or cod.

3 tablespoons mascarpone cheese, at room temperature

½ quantity of Perfect Mashed Potatoes (see page 46)

4 spring onions, thinly sliced

150g (5oz) sun-blush tomatoes, cut into small pieces

Beat the mascarpone cheese into the prepared mash. Carefully stir in the spring onions and tomatoes and serve immediately.

wasabi mashed potatoes

I regularly make horseradish mash, especially as an accompaniment to roast beef for Sunday lunch. It gave me the idea of going one step further and using wasabi – a Japanese horseradish that has a mind-blowing heat. Take great care when adding it to the mash. Remember you can add more but you can't take it away.

This mash is great with all sorts of oriental dishes, as a Fusion alternative to rice or noodles. It's also very good with smoked salmon, believe it or not!

750g (1lb 10oz) floury potatoes, peeled and cut into chunks

50g (2oz) unsalted butter

120ml (4fl oz) hot full-fat milk

2 teaspoons wasabi (Japanese horseradish)

2 tablespoons chopped chives or spring onions

Salt and freshly ground black pepper

Place the potatoes in a pan, cover with cold water, then add a little salt and bring to the boil. Reduce the heat and simmer until tender.

Drain well in a colander and return to the pan. Mash with a potato masher or pass through a potato ricer or sieve.

Beat in the butter with a wooden spoon, then gradually mix in the hot milk. Add the wasabi and beat until fluffy and light. Season to taste and stir in the chives or spring onions.

ratatouille mash with melting olive butter

This dish was created by one of my chefs at the Lanesborough, who inadvertently suggested mixing some ratatouille with creamy mashed potatoes. I tried it and it has now become a popular way of serving mash in the hotel. Great with lamb.

4 tablespoons olive oil

1 small onion, finely chopped

3 garlic cloves, crushed

50g (2oz) aubergine, cut into 1cm (¹/₂ in) dice

¹/₄ red pepper, deseeded and finely diced

¹/₄ yellow pepper, deseeded and finely diced

1 small green courgette, finely diced

1 small yellow courgette, finely diced

1 plum tomato, skinned, deseeded and finely chopped

¹/₂ quantity of Perfect Mashed Potatoes (see page 46)

1 tablespoon chopped basil

¹/₂ teaspoon thyme leaves

Salt and freshly ground black pepper

For the olive butter:

50g (2oz) unsalted butter

1 tablespoon chopped black olives

1 teaspoon lemon juice

For the olive butter, mix the butter with the olives and lemon juice and season to taste. Place the butter on a piece of foil and shape it into a cylinder, wrapping it in the foil. Place in the fridge for 2 hours to firm up.

To make the ratatouille, heat the olive oil in a frying pan, add the onion and garlic and fry until they are just beginning to brown. Add the remaining vegetables and cook over a low heat for 8–10 minutes, until softened. Transfer to a bowl, stir in the mashed potatoes and herbs and season to taste.

Cut the olive butter into slices 5mm (¹/₄ in) thick and arrange on top of the mash. Serve.

golden mash with bourbon and balsamic drizzle

The American way of serving orange sweet potatoes with sweet spices and whisky may sound an unlikely combination but in fact it works extremely well. The vinegar helps to cut the sweetness. Serve with grilled or roast chicken.

750g (1lb 10oz) orange-fleshed sweet potatoes

Juice and finely grated zest of ¹/₂ lemon

A pinch of freshly grated nutmeg

¹/₄ teaspoon ground cinnamon

¹/₄ teaspoon ground allspice

40g (1¹/₂ oz) dark soft brown sugar

4 tablespoons balsamic vinegar, plus a little extra to serve

2 tablespoons bourbon

Salt and freshly ground black pepper

Preheat the oven to 200°C/400F°/gas mark 6. Pierce the potatoes all over with a small, sharp knife, then place on a baking sheet and bake for about 45–50 minutes, until soft. Leave to cool, then cut in half and scoop out the flesh. Transfer to a food processor, add the lemon zest and juice, spices and some salt and process until smooth.

Combine the sugar, vinegar and bourbon in a small pan and bring to the boil. Simmer until it forms a light caramel, then add to the potatoes and mix well. Taste and adjust the seasoning if necessary. Transfer the mash to a serving dish, drizzle over a little balsamic vinegar and serve.

CHARRED ONION AND BACON MASH

Perhaps my favourite mash of all. The smoky flavour of charred red onions and crisp bacon combined with velvety smooth mash – it really tastes as good as it sounds!

2 red onions

3 tablespoons olive oil

150g (5oz) streaky bacon

1 quantity of Perfect Mashed Potatoes (see page 46)

Salt and freshly ground black pepper

Heat a griddle or a ridged grill pan. Peel the onions and cut them into slices 5mm (1/4 in) thick, trying to keep the slices intact. Brush with the olive oil, season with salt and pepper and grill for 5–8 minutes on each side, until charred and tender. Remove from the grill and leave until cool enough to handle, then cut into small dice. Chargrill the bacon for about 4–5 minutes on each side, then chop into small dice also. Add the onion and bacon to the prepared mash and adjust the seasoning. Serve.

CHICKPEA AND OLIVE OIL MASH

125g (4¹/2 oz) chickpeas, soaked in cold water overnight

2 garlic cloves, crushed

¹/2 quantity of Perfect Mashed Potatoes (see page 46)

5 tablespoons fruity olive oil

1 tablespoon sesame oil

A pinch of cayenne pepper

Salt and freshly ground black pepper

Drain the chickpeas, then place them in a pan, cover with fresh water and bring to the boil. Reduce the heat and simmer for 1–1¹/2 hours, until completely tender. Drain, reserving the cooking water. Purée the chickpeas in a blender with the garlic, a little salt and enough of the cooking liquid to give a thick, creamy consistency. Add the purée to the hot mashed potatoes, then beat in the olive oil and sesame oil until they have been absorbed. Adjust the seasoning, transfer to a serving dish and sprinkle over the cayenne pepper.

TRUFFLE, MOREL AND SWEETCORN MASH

A rather gastronomic mash, made with fresh black truffles and wild mushrooms. It's particularly good with chicken and beef.

10g (¹/4 oz) dried morel mushrooms

750g (1lb 10oz) floury potatoes, peeled and cut into chunks

2 corn on the cob, husks removed

150ml (¹/4 pint) full-fat milk

25g (1oz) unsalted butter

1 x 10g (¹/4 oz) fresh black truffle, thinly sliced

100ml (3¹/2 fl oz) double cream

2 slices of white bread, crusts removed, cut into fingers

Salt and freshly ground black pepper

Soak the dried mushrooms in 120ml (4fl oz) hot water for 1 hour, then drain and chop roughly. Set aside.

Place the potatoes in a pan, cover with cold water, then add a little salt and bring to the boil. Reduce the heat and simmer until tender. Meanwhile, using a small, sharp knife, shuck the kernels from the corn cobs. Place in a pan, cover with the milk and bring to the boil. Reduce the heat and simmer for 10–12 minutes, until the corn is tender, then place in a blender and blitz to a smooth purée.

Drain the potatoes in a colander and return to the pan. Mash with a potato masher or pass through a potato ricer or sieve. Stir the sweetcorn purée into the hot mash.

Heat half the butter in a frying pan, add the morels and truffle slices and sauté for 1–2 minutes. Season to taste and mix into the mash. Fold in the cream and adjust the seasoning. Finally, fry the bread fingers in the remaining butter until golden. Put the mash in a serving bowl and top with the fried bread.

CHAMP

According to Irish folklore, this Northern Irish dish should always be made with buttermilk. It is sometimes referred to as stelk or cally.

Put the potatoes in a large pan, cover with cold water, then add a little salt and bring to the boil. Reduce the heat and simmer until just tender. Drain in a colander, return to a low heat and leave to dry out for 2 minutes.

In a separate pan, heat the buttermilk or milk, cream and half the butter. Add the spring onions and cook gently for 5 minutes to remove the raw flavour.

Mash the potatoes until smooth, then, with a wooden spoon, beat in the buttermilk and onion mixture a little at a time to give a light, fluffy consistency. Season to taste, place in a serving dish and make a well in the centre. Add the remaining butter and serve immediately, as the butter slides temptingly down the silky potatoes. Watch your guests dive in in an effort to get a little of that melting butter and soft, fluffy mash.

1kg (2^1/4 lb) floury potatoes, peeled and cut into chunks

200ml (7fl oz) buttermilk or full-fat milk

100ml (3^1/2 fl oz) double cream

75g (3oz) cold unsalted butter, cut into small pieces

A bunch of spring onions, chopped

Salt and freshly ground black pepper

basic potato gnocchi

Here's the Lanesborough's basic recipe for gnocchi, or little potato dumplings, a staple of Italian cuisine. They're very versatile. Try adding mixed herbs, finely chopped cooked mushrooms or other flavourings to the dough.

Serve gnocchi with melted butter, tomato sauce or another sauce of your choice.

900g (2lb) floury potatoes, peeled and cut into chunks
275g (10oz) plain flour
1 egg
Freshly grated nutmeg
Salt and freshly ground black pepper

Place the potatoes in a pan, cover with cold water, add some salt and bring to the boil. Reduce the heat and simmer until tender, then drain well and dry in a clean tea towel. Rub the potatoes through a fine sieve into a large bowl.

Sift in the flour, then add the egg and season with nutmeg, salt and pepper. Mix well and turn out onto a lightly floured work surface. Knead for 2–3 minutes to form a smooth, slightly elastic dough. With floured hands, roll the dough into long cylinders, 2cm (³/4 in) in diameter, then cut into 2cm (³/4 in) lengths. Roll each one lightly over the tines of a fork so it is grooved all over. Place on a floured baking tray until ready to cook.

Bring a large pan of water to the boil, reduce the heat so it is simmering and add the gnocchi in batches, being careful not to crowd the pan. Poach for 3–4 minutes, until the gnocchi rise to the surface. Remove with a slotted spoon, drain well and keep warm in a dish while you cook the rest.

sweet potato gnocchi with red pepper and basil

For the red pepper sauce, heat the olive oil and butter in a pan, add the onion and garlic and cook over a low heat for 3–4 minutes, until softened. Pour in the wine and bring to the boil, then add the chopped peppers and tomato purée and cook for 5–8 minutes. Pour in the stock and return to the boil. Add the herbs and simmer for 20 minutes. Pour the sauce into a blender and blitz until smooth, then season with salt and pepper.

For the gnocchi, preheat the oven to 200°C/400°F/gas mark 6. Place the sweet potatoes on a baking tray and bake until tender. Cut them in half and scoop out the flesh with a spoon. Blitz in a food processor or pass through a sieve to obtain a smooth purée. Place in a bowl, add the egg, flour, 75g (3oz) of the Parmesan and some salt and pepper and mix together thoroughly to form a smooth, fairly firm dough. Shape into classical, Italian gnocchi (see page 51) or simple round balls.

Cook the gnocchi in batches in a large pan of simmering water for 5–8 minutes, until cooked through (cut one open to check), then remove with a slotted spoon and arrange in an ovenproof dish. Put the butter in a pan with 3 tablespoons of water and bring to the boil so the butter melts. Add the chopped basil and simmer for 1 minute, then pour this mixture over the gnocchi. Sprinkle the remaining Parmesan on top and place in an oven preheated to 200°C/400°F/Gas Mark 6 for 5 minutes, until the cheese is bubbling and golden. Reheat the pepper sauce and pour onto 4 plates. Top with the gnocchi and serve.

650g (1lb 6oz) orange-fleshed sweet
    potatoes
1 egg
175g (6oz) plain flour
100g (4oz) Parmesan cheese, freshly grated
75g (3oz) unsalted butter
A good bunch of basil, chopped
Salt and freshly ground black pepper

For the red pepper sauce:
1 tablespoon olive oil
25g (1oz) unsalted butter
1 small onion, chopped
1 garlic clove, crushed
5 tablespoons dry white wine
2 large red peppers, deseeded and chopped
1 tablespoon tomato purée
150ml (1/4 pint) chicken or vegetable stock
A few basil stalks
A sprig of thyme

potato and pumpkin dumplings with horseradish

German-style Knödel such as these are a typical northern European way of making the best of potatoes. They can be served simply with melted butter but I also like to serve them as a garnish for a rich beef and vegetable stew.

Heat half the butter in a frying pan, add the pumpkin cubes and fry until golden all over. Season with salt and pepper and add the water. Reduce the heat, cover the pan and cook until the pumpkin is tender. Leave to cool.

Place the potatoes in a pan, cover with cold water, then add a little salt and bring to the boil. Reduce the heat and simmer until tender, then drain well and mash until smooth. Add the egg yolks, cornflour, semolina, half the flour and the horseradish. Season with nutmeg, salt and pepper and mix well.

Using your hands, shape the mixture into dumplings the size of golf balls, pressing a cube of pumpkin into the centre of each one. Spread the remaining flour over a baking tray or plate and roll the dumplings in it until they are evenly coated.

Put the dumplings in a large, wide pan of boiling salted water, reduce the heat and simmer for 15–20 minutes, until cooked through (cut one open to check). Meanwhile, melt the remaining butter. Remove the dumplings from the pan with a slotted spoon and place in a serving dish. Pour the melted butter over them and serve.

100g (4oz) unsalted butter

125g (4^1/2 oz) peeled pumpkin, cut into 1cm (^{1}/2 in) cubes

100ml (3^1/2 fl oz) water

1.5kg (3lb) floury potatoes, peeled and cut into chunks

3 egg yolks, lightly beaten

3 tablespoons cornflour

3 tablespoons semolina

75g (3oz) plain flour

2 tablespoons freshly grated horseradish

Freshly grated nutmeg

Salt and freshly ground black pepper

potato, Lemon and ricotta pansoti with salsa di noci

Pansoti are a speciality of Liguria in Italy. The name means 'little tummies' – a quirky description of their shape – and classically they are stuffed with a herb filling. My potato, lemon and ricotta filling is equally delicious.

Bake the potatoes until tender (see page 70). Leave until cool enough to handle, then cut them in half, scoop out the flesh into a bowl and crush with a fork. Mix in the ricotta, milk, parsley, lemon zest and cinnamon, season with nutmeg, salt and pepper and leave to cool.

For the pasta dough, place the flour in a large bowl and make a well in the centre. Mix together the wine, water and egg and pour into the well. Carefully fold the flour into the centre and mix thoroughly to form a dough. Turn out and knead for 4–5 minutes, then set aside to rest for 10–15 minutes. Roll out the dough through the stages of a pasta machine, taking it to the narrowest setting, and cut into 7.5cm (3in) triangles. Place a little of the potato filling in the centre of each triangle, brush the edges of the dough with a little water and fold the triangle in half, pressing down firmly to seal.

For the salsa, simmer the walnuts in boiling water for 4–5 minutes, then drain well and peel off the thin brown skin. Put the walnuts, breadcrumbs and Parmesan in a blender, add the ricotta cheese and pine kernels and blend until smooth. Mix in the milk and olive oil and season to taste. Poach the pansoti in a large pan of boiling salted water for about 3–4 minutes, until tender, then drain. Place in a serving dish and pour over the walnut sauce. Sprinkle over the Parmesan cheese and pour around the melted butter.

1kg (2¹/4 lb) red-skinned potatoes
125g (4¹/2 oz) ricotta cheese
2 tablespoons milk
2 tablespoons chopped flat-leaf parsley
Zest of 1 lemon, finely grated
¹/4 teaspoon ground cinnamon
Freshly grated nutmeg
2 tablespoons freshly grated Parmesan cheese
25g (1oz) butter, melted
Salt and freshly ground black pepper

For the pasta dough:
400g (14oz) plain flour
3 tablespoons dry white wine
1 tablespoon water
1 egg

For the salsa di noci:
100g (4oz) walnut halves
50g (2oz) fresh white breadcrumbs
40g (1¹/2 oz) Parmesan cheese, freshly grated
100g (4oz) ricotta cheese
40g (1¹/2 oz) pine kernels
4 tablespoons full-fat milk
4 tablespoons extra virgin olive oil

potato noodles with prawns in their own sauce

Preheat the oven to 200°C/400°F/gas mark 6. Wrap each potato in foil (this makes them softer and easier to peel) and bake until tender, then remove from the foil and peel. Pass the potato flesh through a sieve or a potato ricer into a large bowl. Mix in the Parmesan, flour and some salt and pepper. Make a well in the centre, pour in the eggs and bring together to form a dough. Knead the dough for 1–2 minutes, then wrap in clingfilm and leave to rest for 30 minutes.

Shape the dough into a long roll about 2.5cm (1in) in diameter and cut it into slices about 1cm (^{1}/2 in) thick. Shape them into noodles by rolling each one under the palm of your hand on a floured surface until it is a torpedo shape about 5cm (2in) long. Place on a floured baking tray and set aside.

For the prawns, heat the olive oil in a large pan, add the reserved heads and shells from the prawns and sauté over a high heat for a couple of minutes. Add the chopped vegetables and cook for 4–5 minutes, until softened. Pour in the brandy and wine and boil for 5 minutes, then stir in the tomato purée and cook for a further 5 minutes. Pour over enough water to cover the shells, bring to the boil, then reduce the heat, add the cream and simmer for 10–12 minutes, until the mixture has thickened enough to coat the back of a spoon. Pulverise briefly in a blender or food processor, then strain through a fine sieve into a clean pan. Add the prawns and poach them for 2 minutes in the sauce, until cooked through. Whisk in the chilled butter a few pieces at a time and season to taste. Keep warm.

Poach the potato noodles in a large pan of boiling salted water for 2–3 minutes; they are ready when they rise to the surface. Remove with a slotted spoon, toss with the melted butter and season to taste. Arrange on serving plates and pour over the prawns in their own sauce. Scatter over chervil leaves and serve.

400g (14oz) floury potatoes

50g (2oz) Parmesan cheese, freshly grated

150g (5oz) plain flour

2 eggs, lightly beaten

50g (2oz) unsalted butter, melted

Salt and freshly ground black pepper

Chervil leaves, to garnish

For the prawns:

4 tablespoons olive oil

20 raw tiger prawns, peeled and de-veined (see Tip on page 139) – reserve the heads and shells

100g (4oz) finely chopped mixed carrot, leek and onion

2 tablespoons brandy

100ml (3^1/2 fl oz) dry white wine

1 tablespoon tomato purée

150ml (^{1}/4 pint) double cream

25g (1oz) chilled unsalted butter, cut into small pieces

this chapter

includes some favourite potato basics, such as baked and roast potatoes, as well as a wide range of gratins. The best-known gratin, of course, is the dauphinois (page 60). This dish always provokes controversy but if you bake sliced potatoes slowly in lots of cream you are bound to end up with something delicious whether it's 'authentic' or not. A lovely variation on this is Janssons Frestelse (page 67), a Swedish dish that includes anchovies and onions. The important thing to remember about gratins is to use the right sort of dish – it should be shallow enough to allow the top to brown evenly.

The humble baked potato deserves a more interesting treatment occasionally than the standard knob of butter and sprinkling of grated cheese. It makes a wonderful container for all sorts of flavours – a couple of my favourites are Smoked Cheddar 'Rarebit' Soufflé (page 72) and Cretan Feta, Olive, Toasted Pine Kernels and Oregano (page 71), but the possibilities are endless.

Plain roast potatoes (page 76) are so delicious with the Sunday joint that it's tempting just to leave it at that, but if you fancy a change you will find plenty of other ideas in this chapter to inspire you.

Gratins,
Bakes and
Roasts

Le vrai dauphinois

What makes an authentic gratin dauphinois? It has been a source of debate for years, so perhaps it should come down to individual preference. One thing is agreed, though. On no account should it include cheese – or does that start another dispute?

Preheat the oven to 190°C/375°F/gas mark 5. Peel the potatoes, wipe them dry and slice them thinly lengthways on a mandolin. Take a large, flameproof earthenware dish, rub it lightly with the garlic and then sprinkle with salt. Grease the dish liberally with some of the butter and arrange overlapping slices of potato in it, seasoning between each layer.

Mix the eggs with the cream and milk and pour this mixture over the potatoes to cover them. Dot with the remaining butter. Start cooking the potatoes on top of the stove until the liquid comes to the boil, then place in the oven and cook for 1–1¼ hours, until the potatoes are tender, almost all the liquid has been absorbed and a rich golden crust has formed on the surface. Serve direct from the dish, while very hot.

1kg (2¼ lb) waxy potatoes, such as Maris Peer, Belle de Fontenay or Roseval

2 garlic cloves, crushed

125g (4½ oz) unsalted butter

2 eggs, beaten

300ml (½ pint) double cream

425ml (14fl oz) full-fat milk

Salt and freshly ground black pepper

Crisp crushed potato with goat's cheese, chives and thyme

Preheat the oven to 200°C/400°F/gas mark 6. Cook the potatoes in their skins in boiling salted water until just tender, then drain and leave until cool enough to handle. Peel the potatoes, put them in a bowl and crush lightly with a fork. Mix in the grated goat's cheese, milk, butter and herbs and season with salt and pepper.

Whip the double cream lightly and fold it through the potato mixture. Transfer to a buttered gratin dish and bake for 12–15 minutes, until a golden crust has formed. Serve hot from the oven.

450g (1lb) new potatoes

1 crottin de Chavignol goat's cheese, coarsely grated

5 tablespoons goat's milk

50g (2oz) unsalted butter

1 tablespoon chopped chives

1 teaspoon thyme leaves

100ml (3½ fl oz) double cream

Coarse salt and freshly ground black pepper

BRANDADE OF HALIBUT WITH CRAB GRATIN

Brandade is usually prepared with salt cod but here I have used halibut. What I particularly like about this dish is the crab crust, which makes a lovely crisp topping for the creamed halibut.

Put the milk, cream, garlic, thyme, bay leaf and some salt in a pan and bring to the boil. Reduce the heat to a simmer, add the halibut fillet and poach for 10–12 minutes. Remove the fish with a slotted spoon and place in a large bowl. Add the potatoes to the cooking liquid and simmer until tender. Remove with a slotted spoon, place in another bowl and mash to a purée. Remove the skin from the halibut and add the fish to the mashed potato. Beat in the olive oil and enough of the cooking liquid to form a smooth, creamy brandade. Adjust the seasoning and stir in the chopped chives.

Preheat the oven to 200°C/400°F/gas mark 6. Butter four 10–12cm (4–5in) metal rings, place them on a baking tray and fill with the brandade. Level off the top with a palette knife. Mix together the breadcrumbs, crabmeat and softened butter and sprinkle on top of the brandade. Drizzle over a little olive oil and bake for 12–15 minutes. Meanwhile, prepare a light sauce: put the fish stock in a pan and bring to the boil, then whisk in the butter a few pieces at a time. Add the basil and season to taste.

Place the brandades on serving plates, remove the rings and pour the sauce around. Garnish with basil and serve.

600ml (1 pint) full-fat milk

450ml (¾ pint) double cream

4 garlic cloves, crushed

2 sprigs of thyme

1 bay leaf

650g (1lb 6oz) halibut fillet, skin on

500g (1lb 2oz) floury potatoes, peeled and chopped

6 tablespoons olive oil, plus a little extra for drizzling

4 tablespoons chopped chives

6 tablespoons fresh white breadcrumbs

200g (7oz) fresh white crabmeat

25g (1oz) unsalted butter, softened

Coarse salt and freshly ground black pepper

For the sauce:

150ml (¼ pint) fish stock

50g (2oz) cold unsalted butter, cut into small pieces

10 basil leaves, torn, plus extra to garnish

red potato, onion and herb cheese 'brik'

Briks are a staple of Moroccan cooking, deep-fried parcels of thin, filo-like pastry stuffed with various fillings such as egg, tuna and vegetables. In this recipe, the briks are made using potato slices to replace the pastry. Is this heresy or creativity?

Place the potato slices in a bowl and season with salt and pepper. Melt 75g (3oz) of the butter and pour it over the potatoes while it is still hot. Leave them to soften for about 30 minutes. Meanwhile, carefully mix the diced cheese with the herbs and whipped cream and place in the fridge.

Gently heat the oil in a pan, add the onions and cook for 4–5 minutes, until softened. Add the sugar and cook for 5 minutes, until the onions are caramelised. Remove from the pan and leave to cool.

Heat the remaining butter in a pan, add the Swiss chard and cook for 4–5 minutes, until tender and wilted. Season with salt and pepper.

Preheat the oven to 190°C/375°F/gas mark 5. To assemble the briks, heat 4 blini pans or tartlet tins, 10–12cm (4–5in) in diameter (heating them seals the potato and helps prevent it sticking). Drain excess butter from the softened potatoes and arrange overlapping potato slices inside each mould, letting them overhang the edges. Spread the chard over the base, top with the creamed herb cheese mixture and finally with the caramelised onion. Carefully fold over the overlapping potato to cover the filling. Press down lightly and place on a baking sheet. Bake for 25–30 minutes, until the potatoes are golden, cooked through and crisp. Cool slightly, then turn out onto serving plates and keep warm.

For the sauce, boil the stock and cream together until reduced in volume by a third. Add the herbs, season to taste and pour around the briks.

3 large Desiree potatoes, peeled and cut lengthways into slices 3mm (^{1}/$_8$ in) thick

100g (4oz) unsalted butter

200g (7oz) Neufchâtel cheese, cut into 1cm (^{1}/$_2$ in) dice

2 tablespoons chopped mixed herbs, such as chives, basil, parsley, chervil and tarragon

6 tablespoons double cream, lightly whipped

2 tablespoons olive oil

2 red onions, thinly sliced

1 tablespoon brown sugar

125g (4^1/$_2$ oz) Swiss chard (or spinach), leaves only

Salt and freshly ground black pepper

For the sauce:

150ml (^{1}/$_4$ pint) chicken stock

100ml (3^1/$_2$ fl oz) double cream

1 tablespoon chopped mixed herbs

Red potato 'brik', cooling before being turned out and awaiting its rich herb sauce

GRATIN of New potatoes and Jerusalem artichokes with mustard and Lemon

It's a great pity that Jerusalem artichokes are not as popular as they deserve to be. I love these tuberous little gems, which look like potatoes and can be used in much the same way – deep-fried, boiled or baked, for example. Here they combine wonderfully well with the potatoes in this creamy, mustard-flavoured gratin.

Preheat the oven to 180°C/350°F/gas mark 4. Cook the new potatoes and Jerusalem artichokes in separate pans of boiling salted water for 8–10 minutes, until just tender, then drain in a colander. When they are cool enough to handle, peel the potatoes.

Heat the oil in a frying pan, add the onion, garlic and parsley and cook over a low heat until tender. Add the double cream, mustard and lemon zest and bring to the boil, then season with nutmeg, salt and pepper.

Cut any large potatoes and artichokes in half, leaving smaller ones whole. Place them in a buttered gratin dish, pour over the mustard sauce, sprinkle over the Gruyère and bake for 30 minutes, until golden and bubbling.

450g (1lb) very small new potatoes

200g (7oz) Jerusalem artichokes, peeled

2 tablespoons olive oil

1/2 onion, finely chopped

1 garlic clove, crushed

2 tablespoons chopped parsley

350ml (12fl oz) double cream

1 tablespoon wholegrain mustard

Zest of 1 lemon, finely grated

Freshly grated nutmeg

50g (2oz) Gruyère cheese, grated

Salt and freshly ground black pepper

sweet potato and aubergine lasagne

Here's a meatless lasagne that contains no pasta, replacing it with thinly sliced sweet potatoes instead.

Place the sweet potato slices on an oiled baking sheet and bake for 10–12 minutes, until just soft. Leave to cool. Toss the aubergine slices with the olive oil and garlic and place on a baking sheet. Season and bake for 20 minutes, until just soft, then leave to cool.

For the tomato sauce, heat the oil in a pan, add the onion and garlic and fry until softened. Add the white wine and bring to the boil, then add the tomatoes and bay leaf and simmer for 20 minutes. Season to taste.

For the basil sauce, melt the butter in a pan, stir in the flour and cook gently, stirring, for a few minutes. Gradually stir in the milk, then bring to the boil and simmer gently for a few minutes, until thickened. Season to taste and stir in the basil.

In a bowl, mix together the ricotta, cream, eggs and Parmesan and season to taste.

Preheat the oven to 190°C/375°F/gas mark 5. To assemble the lasagne, spread a third of the tomato sauce over the base of a 25–30cm (10–12in) square earthenware dish, cover with half the sweet potato slices and season well. Add another layer of tomato sauce, followed by half the aubergine. Sprinkle over half the grated Cheddar. Pour over the ricotta mixture and spread evenly, then top with the remaining sweet potato. Spread over the rest of the tomato sauce and top with the remaining aubergine. Pour over the basil sauce. Sprinkle over the last of the Cheddar and bake for 15–20 minutes, until golden and bubbling.

3 white-fleshed sweet potatoes, peeled and cut on the diagonal into slices 5mm (1/4 in) thick

3 large aubergines, cut on the diagonal into slices 1cm (1/2 in) thick

4 tablespoons olive oil

1 garlic clove, crushed

250g (9oz) ricotta cheese

3 tablespoons double cream

2 eggs, beaten

25g (1oz) Parmesan cheese, freshly grated

100g (4oz) Cheddar cheese, grated

Salt and freshly ground black pepper

For the tomato sauce:

1 tablespoon olive oil

1 onion, finely chopped

1 garlic clove, crushed

2 tablespoons white wine

2 x 400g (14oz) cans of tomatoes, chopped

1 bay leaf

For the basil sauce:

25g (1oz) unsalted butter

25g (1oz) plain flour

600ml (1 pint) full-fat milk

3 tablespoons chopped basil

Janssons frestelse (Jansson's temptation)

Legend has it that this Swedish dish tempted a religious fanatic to break his vow to renounce earthly pleasures – hence the name. Whatever, the truth, it's certainly delicious.

Preheat the oven to 190°C/375°F/gas mark 5. Generously butter a gratin dish. Heat the butter in a pan, add the onions, garlic and anchovies and sweat for 8–10 minutes, until tender but not coloured. Layer the potatoes and onion mixture in the gratin dish, adding a grinding of pepper to each layer as you go. Mix the cream and milk together and pour them over the potatoes, which should be completely covered. Cover the dish with foil and bake for 45 minutes. Remove the foil, sprinkle over the breadcrumbs and return to the oven until bubbling and golden. Serve straight from the oven.

25g (1oz) unsalted butter, plus extra for
   greasing the dish

2 onions, thinly sliced

2 garlic cloves, crushed

6 anchovy fillets, chopped

750g (1lb 10oz) waxy potatoes, peeled and
   thinly sliced

600ml (1 pint) double cream

150ml (1/4 pint) full-fat milk

75g (3oz) fresh white breadcrumbs

Freshly ground black pepper

potato and cheese-stuffed chillies rellenos

Preheat the oven to 200°C/400°F/gas mark 6. Cut a slit in the end of each poblano chilli to allow the steam to be released during cooking. Brush the chillies with a little oil and roast in the oven for 5–10 minutes, until the skins are lightly charred and blistered. Place in a polythene bag and seal it. Leave them to steam for 5 minutes, then, using a small knife, carefully peel off the skin. Slit each chilli open from top to bottom and remove the seeds.

Cook the potatoes in boiling salted water until just tender, then drain and place in a bowl. Crush with a fork, mix in the goat's cheese and season to taste. Stuff the chillies with this mixture and arrange them in a single layer in a baking dish.

For the sauce, heat the oil in a frying pan, add the red chillies, garlic and spring onions and cook for a couple of minutes, until softened. Add the tomatoes, corn tortillas, brown sugar and oregano and cook over a gentle heat for 10 minutes. Pour into a blender and blitz to an almost smooth but still slightly textured sauce. Pour the sauce over the stuffed chillies and bake for 10–15 minutes. Scatter with the grated Cheddar, pour over the soured cream and serve.

8 poblano chillies

Vegetable oil, for brushing

350g (12oz) new potatoes, peeled

150g (5oz) firm goat's cheese, crumbled

75g (3oz) Cheddar cheese, grated

4 tablespoons soured cream

Salt and freshly ground black pepper

For the sauce:

4 tablespoons vegetable oil

2 red chillies, deseeded and chopped

2 garlic cloves, crushed

4 spring onions, chopped

400g (14oz) can of tomatoes, chopped

4 corn tortillas, chopped

2 tablespoons brown sugar

1 tablespoon chopped oregano

Potato and cheese-stuffed chillies rellenos, before sauce has been poured over, prior to baking

the ultimate baked potato

4 large, floury potatoes
4 tablespoons coarse sea salt
50g (2oz) unsalted butter
Freshly cracked black pepper

Preheat the oven to 200°C/400°F/gas mark 6. Using a small brush, scrub the potatoes thoroughly under running water to remove any dirt. Pat them dry, then prick the skins all over with a small knife. Scatter the coarse salt into a baking tin and place the potatoes on top. Bake for 1–1¼ hours, depending on size, until tender.

Remove the potatoes from the oven, cut a cross in the top of each one and squeeze the potato gently to open it out. Top with the butter, cracked black pepper and sea salt.

the ultimate baked potato

baked potato fillings

Leek, mustard and parsley

4 large, floury potatoes

3 tablespoons olive oil

1 large leek, finely chopped

2 tablespoons grain mustard

100g (4oz) mature Cheddar cheese, grated

4 tablespoons double cream

25g (1oz) unsalted butter

3 tablespoons chopped flat-leaf parsley

Salt and freshly ground black pepper

Bake the potatoes until tender (see page 70), then cut a lid off each one. Carefully scoop out the flesh, leaving a thin shell, and put it into a bowl.

Heat the olive oil in a pan, add the leek and cook over a low heat for 8–10 minutes, until tender. Add the leek to the potato flesh with the mustard, Cheddar and cream and mix well. Finally mix in the butter and parsley. Season to taste, then return the mixture to the potato shells and reheat in the oven for a few minutes before serving.

cretan feta, olive, toasted pine kernels and oregano

4 large, floury potatoes

50g (2oz) unsalted butter

4 tablespoons olive oil

100g (4oz) Greek feta cheese, cut into 5mm (1/4 in) cubes

2 tablespoons currants, soaked in hot water for 30 minutes and then drained

2 tablespoons pine kernels, toasted

6 green olives, pitted and chopped

2 tablespoons chopped oregano

Salt and freshly ground black pepper

Bake the potatoes until tender (see page 70), then cut a lid off each one. Carefully scoop out the flesh into a bowl, add the butter and oil and mash lightly. Gently fold in the remaining ingredients. Fill the potato shells with the mixture and return to the oven for 5–6 minutes to heat through before serving.

mozzarella, basil and sun-blush tomatoes

4 large, floury potatoes

8 garlic cloves

2 tablespoons olive oil

4 good handfuls of basil leaves, roughly chopped

100g (4oz) sun-blush tomatoes, cut into small pieces

250g (9oz) buffalo mozzarella, cut into 5mm (1/4 in) dice

Salt and freshly ground black pepper

Bake the potatoes until tender (see page 70). Meanwhile, place the unpeeled garlic cloves in a baking tin, pour over the oil and roast in the oven for 25–30 minutes, until golden and caramelised. Remove the skins and mash the flesh coarsely in a bowl. Add the basil, mozzarella and tomatoes and season lightly.

Make an incision or a cross in the centre of each potato and open it up. Fill with the cheese and tomato mixture and return to the oven for 8–10 minutes, until the mozzarella is bubbling.

BAKED POTATO FILLINGS

DOLCELATTE, SPRING ONION AND CHIVES

4 large, floury potatoes

150g (5oz) dolcelatte cheese

4 tablespoons double cream

50g (2oz) unsalted butter

2 egg yolks

1 tablespoon chopped chives

6 spring onions, shredded

Salt and freshly ground black pepper

Bake the potatoes until tender (see page 70), then cut a lid off each one. Carefully scoop out the flesh into a bowl and mash while hot. Add the dolcelatte, cream and butter and blend well. Mix in the egg yolks, chives, spring onions and some seasoning, then fill the potato shells with the mixture. Return to the oven until golden.

ASPARAGUS, WILD MUSHROOM, PECORINO AND BAKED EGGS

4 large, floury potatoes

50g (2oz) unsalted butter

6 medium asparagus spears

2 tablespoons olive oil

75g (3oz) trompette de la mort mushrooms (or other wild mushrooms), cut into large dice

4 eggs

4 tablespoons double cream

75g (3oz) pecorino cheese, grated

Salt and freshly ground black pepper

Bake the potatoes until tender (see page 70), then cut a lid off each one. Carefully scoop out the flesh into a bowl and mash lightly with the butter.

Blanch the asparagus in boiling water for 3 minutes, then drain well and chop. Heat the olive oil in a pan, add the asparagus and mushrooms and sauté over a medium heat for 2–3 minutes. Add to the potatoes and season to taste. Fill the potato shells with the mixture and then press it down with the back of a spoon to create a hollow in the centre of each one.

Crack an egg into each hollow, pour over a tablespoon of cream and sprinkle with the grated pecorino. Season with salt and pepper. Replace the lids and return the potatoes to the oven for 10–12 minutes, until the eggs have just set.

SMOKED CHEDDAR 'RAREBIT' SOUFFLÉ

4 large, floury potatoes

25g (1oz) unsalted butter

25g (1oz) plain flour

150ml (1/4 pint) full-fat milk

4 tablespoons beer

1 teaspoon English mustard

2 drops of Worcestershire sauce

125g (4 1/2 oz) smoked Cheddar cheese, grated

3 eggs, separated

1 tablespoon chopped chives

Salt and freshly ground black pepper

Bake the potatoes until tender (see page 70), then cut a lid off each one. Carefully scoop out the flesh into a bowl and mash until smooth.

Melt the butter in a pan, add the flour and cook for 1 minute. Gradually stir in the milk and bring to the boil to make a thick sauce. Add the beer, mustard and Worcestershire sauce, then stir in the grated cheese and cook very gently for 2–3 minutes, until it has melted. Season with salt and pepper. Stir this sauce into the mashed potato, then add the egg yolks and adjust the seasoning. Whisk the egg whites until stiff, then gently fold them into the potato mixture with a metal spoon.

Carefully fill the potato shells with the soufflé mixture. Return to the oven and bake for 25 minutes, until golden and risen. Garnish with chopped chives and serve.

soured cream, smoked mackerel and horseradish

4 large, floury potatoes

2 egg yolks

4 tablespoons soured cream

2 tablespoons creamed horseradish

150g (5oz) smoked mackerel fillet, skinned

A small handful of rocket leaves, roughly chopped

Salt and freshly ground black pepper

Bake the potatoes until tender (see page 70), then cut a lid off each one. Carefully scoop out the flesh into a bowl and mash until smooth. Beat in the egg yolks, soured cream and horseradish. Flake the smoked mackerel into pieces and mix with the potato, then add the rocket leaves and season with salt and pepper. Fill the potato shells with the mixture and return to the oven for 5–6 minutes, until golden.

mini jacket potatoes with soured cream and caviar

A simple yet extravagant pre-drinks appetiser. It's also good served with grilled fish.

24 small new potatoes

2 tablespoons chopped chives

100ml (3¹/₂ fl oz) soured cream

10g (¹/₄ oz) Sevruga caviar

Bake the potatoes until tender (see page 70) – they will take 20–30 minutes, depending on size. Then, with a small knife, make a cross in the top of each potato and use your thumbs and forefingers to squeeze it gently open. Mix together the chives and soured cream and spoon a dollop onto each potato. Top with the caviar and serve immediately.

moroccan baked potato skins

Here's a tasty snack with a spicy touch, although it's not really authentically Moroccan – I like to sprinkle some grated Cheddar over the potato skins during the final few minutes of cooking.

Preheat the oven to 220°C/425°F/gas mark 7. Cut the skin off the potatoes so it is about 2cm (3/4 in) thick, wash it thoroughly and dry well. Place in a large baking dish.

Mix together all the remaining ingredients except the cheese, pour over the skins and toss well together. Place in the oven and bake for about 35 minutes, until golden and crisp. Sprinkle over the Cheddar cheese and return to the oven until melted and bubbling.

650g (1lb 6oz) large floury potatoes

100ml (3^1/$_2$ fl oz) olive oil

1 tablespoon good-quality harissa paste

^{1}/$_2$ teaspoon ground cumin

^{1}/$_2$ teaspoon ground coriander

^{1}/$_2$ teaspoon ground cinnamon

^{1}/$_4$ teaspoon turmeric

2 garlic cloves, crushed

75g (3oz) Cheddar cheese, grated

Salt and freshly ground black pepper

As with all simple things, it's worth taking the trouble to get these right. Here are a few tips to help you make perfect roast potatoes.

- Floury potatoes such as Maris Piper, Cara, Desiree and King Edward produce a fluffy interior, while waxy varieties give a smoother texture. I prefer to use floury potatoes but both are good.
- Peel the potatoes just before cooking them; don't leave them soaking in water.
- Parboiling the potatoes before roasting breaks down their structure, which means that the cooking time is reduced and the outside becomes crisper.
- Make sure the oil in the roasting tin is very hot (almost smoking) before adding the potatoes but don't allow it to burn. If the oil isn't hot enough, the potatoes will be greasy.
- For really crisp potatoes, make sure they are completely dry before adding them to the hot oil.
- Don't turn the potatoes until they are golden on one side.
- Season the potatoes only when they are cooked; otherwise the salt will make them mushy.
- Serve roast potatoes as soon as they are ready, so they don't lose their crispness.
- I like to cook roast potatoes alongside the meat so they absorb some of the flavour. However, the meat juices can make them slightly soggy. If you like really crisp potatoes, roast them in a separate tin.

roast potatoes

750g (1lb 10oz) floury potatoes, peeled and cut into large, even-sized pieces
4 tablespoons vegetable oil (or fat from the roast)
Salt and freshly ground black pepper

Preheat the oven to 200°C/400°F/gas mark 6. Place the potatoes in a large pan, cover with cold water, then add a pinch of salt and bring to the boil. Reduce the heat and simmer for 10–15 minutes, until almost tender. Drain in a colander and leave for 5 minutes to dry.

Heat the oil in a large roasting tin until very hot. Add the potatoes to the hot oil and turn to coat them evenly. Roast in the oven for 30–40 minutes, until golden and crisp, turning them halfway through. Season with salt and pepper and then serve.

tip

TO PREPARE YOUR OWN FRAGRANT GARLIC SALT, separate the cloves of 1 head of garlic, peel them and slice thinly on a mandolin. Spread the garlic out on a non-stick baking sheet and bake in an oven preheated to 150°C/200°F/gas mark 2 for 3–4 hours, until withered and dry. Leave to cool, then place in a food processor or blender with 100g (4oz) coarse sea salt and blitz for 30 seconds to combine. Do not overprocess or the salt will be too fine. Stored in an airtight container, this should keep indefinitely.

variations

- *Add 1 tablespoon dried or fresh herbs to the potatoes before placing them in the oven.*
- *Add a favourite spice, such as Cajun seasoning, paprika or garlic salt (see Tip above).*

roast potatoes with herbes de provence

Generally I am not keen on using dried herbs but when roasting potatoes like this I make an exception to the rule. These potatoes are very good served with lamb cutlets that have been marinated for about an hour in a mixture of olive oil, crushed garlic, rosemary and orange zest, then grilled.

Preheat the oven to 220°C/425°F/gas mark 7. Cut the unpeeled potatoes in half lengthways, then score the flesh-side of each half in a criss-cross fashion. Arrange on a baking tray, cut-side up. Pour over the olive oil, season with salt and pepper and sprinkle over the dried herbs. Roast in the oven for 45–50 minutes, until tender, golden and crisp.

12 medium baking potatoes

4 tablespoons olive oil

1 teaspoon dried herbes de Provence

Coarse salt and freshly ground black pepper

roast red-skinned potatoes with chilli and horseradish crème fraîche

Preheat the oven to 200°C/400°F/gas mark 6. Place the whole, unpeeled potatoes in a large roasting tin, pour over the olive oil and toss well. Season with salt and pepper and tuck in the fresh thyme. Roast for 35–40 minutes, until tender and golden, then allow to cool slightly. Meanwhile, mix together the horseradish, crème fraîche, chilli and chives and season to taste. Cut the potatoes in half, arrange on a serving plate and top with the chilli and horseradish crème fraîche.

500g (1lb 2oz) baby red potatoes

4 tablespoons olive oil

8 sprigs of thyme

2 tablespoons freshly grated horseradish root

100ml (3¹/₂ fl oz) crème fraîche

1 large red chilli, deseeded and chopped

2 tablespoons chopped chives

Salt and freshly ground black pepper

roast sweet potatoes with cardamom, chilli and cinnamon

Preheat the oven to 200°C/400°F/gas mark 6. In a bowl, toss the sweet potatoes with the cracked cardamom, cloves, cinnamon stick and bay leaves. Heat the oil and half the butter in an ovenproof frying pan, add the sweet potatoes and spices and toss in the hot fat for 5 minutes. Transfer to the oven and roast for 30–35 minutes, until the potatoes are tender and golden.

Remove the spices from the potatoes, add the remaining butter, the chilli sauce and some salt and toss well.

600g (1lb 5oz) orange-fleshed sweet
    potatoes, peeled and cut into 1cm (1/2 in)
    dice
6 black cardamom pods, cracked (see Tip)
3 cloves
1 cinnamon stick
2 small bay leaves
2 tablespoons vegetable oil
50g (2oz) unsalted butter
2 tablespoons hot chilli sauce
Salt

tip

ALTHOUGH YOU CAN BUY READY-GROUND CARDAMOM it tends to lose its flavour very quickly. I've found the best and quickest way to grind your own is to place whole pods in a blender or food processor and blitz for 30 seconds. Transfer to a fine sieve and sift the ground seeds through, leaving the pods behind.

roast tikka masala potatoes

Preheat the oven to 200°C/400°F/gas mark 6. Cook the potatoes in a pan of boiling salted water for 5–8 minutes, until they are just tender but still with a bite. Drain them in a colander.

Melt the ghee or clarified butter in a roasting tin on the hob, add the mustard seeds and fry until they begin to pop. Add the coriander seeds, cardamom pods, nigella seeds, ginger, chilli, curry leaves and turmeric and cook for 2 minutes. Add the potatoes and stir to coat them in the spices. Add the water and stir again. Place in the oven and roast for 20–25 minutes, until the potatoes are golden and crusty with the spices. Season to taste and serve immediately.

650g (1lb 5oz) small waxy potatoes, whole or
    halved, depending on size, and peeled
75g (3oz) ghee or clarified butter (see Tip on
    page 153)
1/2 teaspoon black mustard seeds
1 teaspoon coriander seeds, toasted briefly
    in a dry frying pan
8 black cardamom pods, cracked (see Tip)
1/4 teaspoon nigella seeds (black onion seeds)
2.5cm (1in) piece of fresh root ginger, finely
    chopped
1 green chilli, deseeded and thinly sliced
6 fresh curry leaves
A pinch of turmeric
100ml (3 1/2 fl oz) water
Salt and freshly ground black pepper

Roast tikka masala potatoes straight from the oven

BAY-STUDDED POTATOES WITH ROSEMARY AND OLIVE OIL

Preheat the oven to 200°C/400°F/gas mark 6. With a small knife, cut each potato across its width in slices about 1cm (1/2 in) thick, stopping 1cm (1/2 in) before the bottom so the slices are still joined at the base. Season with salt and pepper and insert a few bay leaves in the cuts in each potato. Place the potatoes in a roasting tin, pour over the oil and brush with a little of the melted butter. Roast in the oven for 30–40 minutes, until tender.

Brush with the remaining butter, scatter the rosemary over the top and return to the oven for 10–15 minutes, until golden. Drain and sprinkle with coarse salt.

VARIATION

Add 100g (4oz) pancetta, cut into lardons, and some whole peeled garlic cloves to the roasting tin before pouring over the oil.

8 large new potatoes

16 bay leaves

3 tablespoons olive oil

75g (3oz) unsalted butter, melted

4 sprigs of rosemary

Coarse salt and freshly ground black pepper

WHO CAN RESIST fried potatoes, in
any shape or form? Crisp, succulent and unbelievably
moreish, they might have been designed expressly to tempt
us from healthy eating resolutions. In fact, they aren't
necessarily as high in fat as you might think. As long as the
cooking oil is the correct temperature, the potatoes should
be sealed quickly and won't absorb too much of it. Deep-
fried potatoes should always be drained well on kitchen
paper before serving, to avoid greasiness.

This chapter explains how to make perfect sauté potatoes
and chips, with several variations on the theme. Sauté
potatoes can be a sophisticated accompaniment to grilled
meat and fish, but I think they come into their own as simple
breakfast or brunch dishes, such as Bubble and Squeak (page
86), Sauté Potatoes with Tomato Tapenade and Fried Egg
(page 85) or a new twist on hash browns (page 88).

Like so many potato dishes, fritters and potato cakes
make an ideal vehicle for other flavours. They work particularly
well with Indian spices – try the Aloo Tikki (page 98) – but
also have a real affinity with Mediterranean ingredients.

sautés, fritters, potato cakes and chips

sauté potatoes

650g (1lb 6oz) medium-sized waxy new
    potatoes
4 tablespoons vegetable oil
25g (1oz) unsalted butter
1 tablespoon chopped parsley (optional)
Salt and freshly ground black pepper

Cook the whole, unpeeled potatoes in boiling salted water until almost tender. Drain in a colander and leave until cool enough to handle, then carefully peel off the skins. Cut the potatoes into slices roughly 1cm ($^1/_2$ in) thick.

    Heat the oil in a large frying pan, add the potatoes and fry quickly to develop the colour; avoid turning or tossing them until they are crisp and browned underneath. Add the butter and, when it is foaming gently, toss it with the potatoes until they become beautifully golden in colour. Season with salt and pepper, then place in a serving dish and sprinkle with chopped parsley, if using.

cLassic Lyonnaise potatoes

Sauté 1 thinly sliced onion in butter until golden and caramelised, then stir it into the sauté potatoes before adding the seasoning. Lyonnaise potatoes used to be made with puréed onion, but now sautéed onion is the norm.

sauté potatoes with juniper berries, rosemary and emmenthal

1 teaspoon juniper berries
1 quantity of Sauté Potatoes (see left)
1 tablespoon chopped rosemary
40g (1$^1/_2$ oz) Emmenthal cheese, cut into
    5mm ($^1/_4$ in) cubes
Salt and freshly ground black pepper

Put the juniper berries in a mortar and crush to a fine powder. Make the sauté potatoes in the usual way but after adding the butter, season them with the juniper along with salt and pepper. Sprinkle over the rosemary and cheese, toss together quickly and transfer to a serving dish.

IRRESISTIBLE sauté potatoes

patatas catalan

1 red pepper, halved and deseeded

4 tablespoons olive oil

75g (3oz) chorizo or merguez sausage, roughly chopped

1 garlic clove, crushed

12 black olives

1 quantity of Sauté Potatoes (see page 84)

1 tablespoon chopped parsley

Salt and freshly ground black pepper

Preheat the oven to 200°C/400°F/ gas mark 6. Place the pepper halves on a baking sheet, coat with half the olive oil and roast for 20–25 minutes, until blistered and blackened. Leave to cool, then peel off the skin and cut the pepper into long strips.

Heat the remaining oil in a frying pan, add the sausage and garlic and fry for 1 minute, until the sausage is crisp and golden.

Add the red pepper and olives and toss together. Add the sauté potatoes, toss and adjust the seasoning. Garnish with parsley.

sauté potatoes with crisp artichokes and wilted rocket

3 small globe artichokes

4 tablespoons olive oil

50g (2oz) young rocket leaves

6 basil leaves

1 quantity of Sauté Potatoes (see page 84)

Salt and freshly ground black pepper

Break the stalks off the artichokes, then slice off the tops. Pull off and discard the tough, dark outer leaves. Cut the artichokes in half to expose the choke (hairy fibres). Quickly scrape out the choke, then cut the artichokes into slices 1cm (1/2 in) thick.

Heat the oil in a large frying pan, add the artichokes and cook for 2 minutes. Add the rocket and basil leaves and cook for 1 minute, until wilted, then mix in the sauté potatoes. Adjust the seasoning and serve.

sauté potatoes with tomato tapenade and fried egg

Everybody loves fried eggs and potatoes. In this recipe, I go one step further and top them with a piquant tomato relish. I also use the relish as a dip for bread and get regular requests for it from guests.

2 tablespoons olive oil

4 free-range eggs

1 quantity of Sauté Potatoes (see page 84)

50g (2oz) Parmesan cheese shavings

For the tomato tapenade:

50g (2oz) sun-dried tomatoes

20g (3/4 oz) baby capers

20g (3/4 oz) green olives, pitted

1 large garlic clove, crushed

1 teaspoon chopped rosemary

1/2 teaspoon lemon juice

2 tablespoons olive oil

For the tapenade, put all the ingredients in a blender or small food processor and blitz to a coarse purée, then set aside.

Heat the oil in a frying pan and fry the eggs. Spoon the tapenade onto the sauté potatoes, arrange the eggs on top and garnish with Parmesan shavings. Serve.

tip

THE TOMATO TAPENADE KEEPS WELL in the fridge and in fact is better when left for a day or two so the flavours can infuse.

Quail's eggs make a nice change from hen's eggs, cooked in the same way.

bubble and squeak

Until recently bubble and squeak was only cooked at home, an ideal way of using up leftover potatoes, but now it regularly appears on restaurant menus. Its name supposedly comes from the noise the ingredients make in the pan. The cabbage can be replaced with other ingredients, such as Brussels sprouts and spinach. The addition of a little crisp bacon, although not traditional, is very good.

2 tablespoons olive oil

40g (1¹/2 oz) unsalted butter

1 onion, finely chopped

2 garlic cloves, crushed

100g (4oz) cooked Savoy cabbage, roughly chopped

450g (1lb) boiled potatoes, peeled

Salt and freshly ground black pepper

Heat the oil and butter in a large frying pan, add the onion and garlic and sauté until tender. Add the cabbage, season well and toss with the onion and garlic. Now add the cooked potatoes and crush with a fork. Toss together until lightly browned, then season to taste and serve.

potato cubes with crispy bacon and herb gremolata

tip

ALWAYS USE YOUR OWN FRESH WHITE BREADCRUMBS rather than buying the commercial variety that look and taste like sawdust. To make your own, simply place the bread (crusts removed) in a food processor or blender and blitz to a fine texture – simple as that!

Place the potatoes in a pan, cover with cold water, then add a little salt and bring to the boil. Reduce the heat and simmer until the potatoes are almost but not quite cooked. Drain in a colander and cool slightly.

Mix together the herbs, lemon zest and breadcrumbs and season with salt and pepper. Season the potatoes, then dip them in the beaten egg whites and coat in the herb crumbs.

Heat a dry frying pan, add the bacon and fry for 2–3 minutes, until golden and crisp. Remove with a slotted spoon and keep warm. Add the oil to the pan, followed by the potatoes, and fry until golden all over. Return the bacon to the pan, toss with the potatoes and serve.

650g (1lb 6oz) small baking potatoes, peeled and cut into 1cm (¹/2 in) cubes

4 tablespoons chopped mixed herbs, such as tarragon, parsley and chives

Zest of ¹/2 lemon, finely grated

100g (4oz) fresh white breadcrumbs

2 egg whites, lightly beaten

125g (4¹/2 oz) smoked bacon, chopped into small pieces

3 tablespoons vegetable oil

Salt and freshly ground black pepper

Potato cubes with crispy bacon and herb gremolata

CYPRIOT HASH BROWNS WITH HALOUMI IN PITTA BREAD

Hash browns is the American name for crisp fried potatoes. Outside America they tend to be made with grated cooked potato. Americans, however, prefer more rustic diced potatoes. In this recipe I use them as part of a great sandwich with Cypriot cheese.

Put the unpeeled potatoes in a pan, cover with cold water, add a little salt and bring to the boil. Reduce the heat and simmer until tender, then drain and leave to cool. Peel the potatoes and cut them into 1cm (1/2 in) dice. Place in a bowl, add the onion, oregano, garlic and olives, then season with salt and pepper.

Whisk together all the ingredients for the dressing and season to taste.

Heat half the oil in a large frying pan until very hot, add the potato mixture and fry until the potatoes are crisp, tossing them as you cook; they should be brown and crusty all over. Remove from the heat and keep warm.

Heat a ridged grill pan until smoking. Dip the haloumi slices in the remaining oil, season and then chargrill for 1–2 minutes, until golden and lightly charred on both sides.

Grill the pitta breads until warm, then split them open. Fill with the hash brown mix, then lay the slices of grilled haloumi on top. Drizzle over the dressing, close the lid, cut in half and enjoy!

450g (1lb) floury potatoes

1 red onion, chopped

1 tablespoon chopped oregano

1 garlic clove, crushed

10 black olives, pitted and chopped

6 tablespoons olive oil

12 slices of haloumi cheese

4 pitta breads

Salt and freshly ground black pepper

For the dressing:

4 tablespoons olive oil

Juice of 1 lemon

1 tablespoon superfine capers, rinsed and drained

2 tablespoons sherry vinegar

1 tablespoon chopped chives

tortilla basquaise

Heat the oil in a 20cm (8in) omelette pan, add the potatoes and fry for 2–3 minutes, until sealed on both sides. Add the onion and cook until both onion and potato are golden. Season with salt and pepper and add the chorizo. Cover with a lid and cook over a low heat for 20 minutes or until tender, stirring occasionally.

Beat the eggs with the saffron water and a little seasoning. Pour over the potato mixture and spread out evenly. Cook over a low heat, uncovered, for 8–10 minutes, until just set (if necessary, put the pan under a hot grill for a minute or two to set the top). Gently run a palette knife around the edge of the tortilla to loosen the edges, then invert the tortilla onto a plate. Allow to cool before cutting into wedges. Serve with a crisp green salad.

4 tablespoons good-quality olive oil

400g (14oz) Desiree potatoes, peeled and thinly sliced

1 onion, thinly sliced

75g (3oz) chorizo, skinned and thinly sliced

5 large eggs

A pinch of saffron strands, soaked in 2 tablespoons hot water

Salt and freshly ground black pepper

caramelised potatoes with tomato, thyme and marjoram

I have always had rather a sweet tooth so this potato dish hits the right note in my estimation. It makes the most of the flavours of southern France, the sweet sun-blush tomatoes working particularly well with the garlic and highly perfumed marjoram. Try serving these potatoes as an accompaniment to a plain roast leg of lamb.

Scrub the potatoes well under cold running water, then dry thoroughly on a kitchen towel. Heat the olive oil in a large, heavy-based frying pan, add the potatoes and cook over a medium heat for 15–20 minutes, until lightly browned all over and almost tender. Reduce the heat and add the butter, herbs, garlic, chilli and tomatoes. Cook for 3–4 minutes, tossing the potatoes continually. Finally, sprinkle over the sugar and cook for 1–2 minutes longer, until the potatoes are caramelised. Adjust the seasoning and serve.

1kg (2¼ lb) small new potatoes, preferably Jersey Royal

6 tablespoons olive oil

50g (2oz) unsalted butter

3 sprigs of thyme

3 sprigs of marjoram

3 garlic cloves, crushed

1 small red chilli, deseeded and finely chopped

100g (4oz) sun-blush tomatoes, chopped

2 teaspoons caster sugar

Salt and freshly ground black pepper

tip

SUN-BLUSH TOMATOES are sweet, semi-dried tomatoes marinated in oil and herbs. You should be able to find them in delis and some supermarkets.

pan-fried potato and fruit terrine

This unusual terrine goes particularly well with slices of baked gammon or with game. It's best made a day or two before you need it. Not only does this enhance the flavour but it also makes it easier to slice before frying.

I first published this recipe in The Complete Masterchefs *(Weidenfeld & Nicolson) two years ago. Since then I have streamlined it slightly and just couldn't leave it out of this collection of potato recipes.*

Serves 8–10

Preheat the oven to 180°C/350°F/gas mark 4. Stretch the bacon rashers by running the back of a knife along each one, then use them to line a 900g (2lb) loaf tin or terrine dish, overlapping them slightly and letting them overhang the top of the tin.

Heat the olive oil in a frying pan, add the onion and sauté until golden. Transfer to a plate and leave to cool. Peel the potatoes and grate them coarsely. Put them in a tea towel and squeeze out excess liquid, then put them into a large bowl. Add the onion, dried fruit, eggs, cream, potato flour and finally the cheese. Mix well and season with nutmeg, salt and pepper. Pack the mixture into the bacon-lined loaf tin and fold the overlapping bacon over the top. Cover with a piece of lightly greased foil, place in the oven and cook for about 1¹/₂ hours, until soft when tested with a skewer. Leave to cool, then place in the fridge to set firm.

To serve, turn the terrine out and cut it into slices 2cm (³/4 in) thick. Fry in the butter until golden and slightly crisp.

450g (1lb) streaky bacon rashers, rind removed

4 tablespoons olive oil

1 onion, finely chopped

675g (1¹/2 lb) waxy potatoes

125g (4¹/2 oz) mixed dried fruit, such as prunes, apples and apricots, cut into 2cm (³/4 in) dice

3 eggs

100ml (3¹/2 fl oz) double cream

2 tablespoons potato flour (or arrowroot)

150g (5oz) Beaufort or Gruyère cheese, cut into 1cm (¹/2 in) cubes

Freshly grated nutmeg

25g (1oz) unsalted butter

Salt and freshly ground black pepper

crispy potato and goat's cheese ricotta fritters

Light, feathery and cheesy – potato fritters that everyone will love. I like to serve these as a vegetarian starter. If you can't find goat's cheese ricotta, ordinary ricotta will be fine.

450g (1lb) floury potatoes, peeled and cut into chunks

40g (1^1/2 oz) unsalted butter

2 egg yolks

120ml (4fl oz) water

50g (2oz) plain flour, sifted

2 eggs

150g (5oz) goat's cheese ricotta

Oil, for deep-frying

Salt and freshly ground black pepper

Put the potatoes in a pan, cover with water, add a little salt and bring to the boil. Reduce the heat and simmer until tender, then drain well in a colander. Return the potatoes to the pan and dry them out over a low heat. Mash with 15g (^{1}/2 oz) of the butter until smooth and then beat in the egg yolks. Keep warm.

Dice the remaining butter and put it in a pan with the water and a little salt. Bring to the boil so the butter melts, then gently rain in the flour and beat with a spatula until the mixture is smooth and leaves the sides of the pan clean. Reduce the heat to a minimum and cook for 1 minute, beating constantly. Remove from the heat and allow to cool slightly, then beat in the eggs one at a time. Mix in the mashed potato mixture and then add the ricotta. Beat well together and season to taste.

Heat some oil to 160°C/325°F in a deep-fat fryer or a large, deep saucepan. Take some of the potato mixture in an oiled dessertspoon, drop it into the hot oil and fry a few at a time for 3–4 minutes, until puffed up and golden. Remove with a slotted spoon and drain on kitchen paper. Sprinkle with salt and serve.

tip

THESE FRITTERS ARE PARTICULARLY GOOD served with a tart tomato or apple chutney and garnished with rocket leaves.

spicy potato fritters

These Indian-style potato fritters are made with sliced white sweet potatoes dipped in a delicate spicy batter and fried until crisp. The kachumber salad makes an ideal accompaniment.

Put the gram flour, garam masala, mustard seeds, turmeric, cumin seeds and baking powder in a bowl and mix well. Stir in enough iced water to make a thick batter, then add the chillies, spring onions and coriander. Leave to rest for 20 minutes.

For the salad mix the tomatoes, red onion, chilli, garlic, oil and lemon juice in a dish and season to taste. Arrange on a serving plate, scatter over the chopped coriander and leave to stand at room temperature for 30 minutes.

Heat the oil to 180°C/350°F in a deep-fat fryer or a deep saucepan. Dip the potato slices in the batter and fry in batches for about 3–4 minutes, until golden, turning them as they cook. Remove with a slotted spoon and drain on kitchen paper. Serve hot with the kachumber salad.

150g (5oz) gram flour (chickpea flour)

1 tablespoon garam masala

$1/2$ teaspoon black mustard seeds

$1/2$ teaspoon turmeric

1 teaspoon cumin seeds, toasted briefly in a dry frying pan and then crushed

$1/2$ teaspoon baking powder

Iced water, to mix

2 green jalapeño chillies, deseeded and finely chopped

3 spring onions, finely chopped

1 tablespoon chopped coriander

Vegetable oil, for deep-frying

3 white-fleshed sweet potatoes, peeled and cut into slices 3mm ($1/8$ in) thick

For the kachumber salad:

2 beefsteak tomatoes, sliced

1 small red onion, thinly sliced

1 green jalapeño chilli, deseeded and finely chopped

1 garlic clove, crushed

4 teaspoons groundnut oil or olive oil

Juice of $1/2$ lemon

1 tablespoon chopped coriander

Salt and freshly ground black pepper

potato kibbeh with Lamb, feta and mint

Kibbeh is a Middle Eastern dish traditionally made of finely minced meat mixed with onion, spices and cracked wheat. There are lots of variations throughout the Middle East – for example, the Egyptians prefer to replace the wheat with ground rice. Here's a potato version of kibbeh with a meat filling, plus a couple more variations on the theme.

Place the cracked wheat in a bowl, pour over the boiling water and leave for 20–25 minutes, until the water has been absorbed and the wheat is swollen and fluffy. Leave to cool, then mix with the mashed potato, egg, melted butter, spices and some salt and pepper. Place in the fridge while preparing the filling.

Heat the olive oil in a frying pan until smoking hot. Season the lamb and fry in the hot oil with the ground allspice for 10–15 minutes, until cooked through. Transfer to a bowl. Heat the butter in the same pan, add the onion and pine kernels and cook until golden. Add to the meat in the bowl and leave to cool, then stir in the feta and mint. Divide the potato mixture into 12 portions and shape them into small patties. Place a little of the lamb stuffing in the centre of each one and then reshape the potato into an oval so the filling is completely enclosed. Heat some vegetable oil to 180°C/350°F in a deep-fat fryer or a deep saucepan and fry the kibbeh until golden and slightly puffy. Drain on kitchen paper and serve.

variations

Fill the potato mixture with one of the following instead of lamb:
- *Finely chopped cooked spinach bound with cream cheese.*
- *Spicy sauté potatoes and pitted, chopped olives.*

100g (4oz) cracked wheat (bulgur)

200ml (7fl oz) boiling water

300g (11oz) mashed potato (made without any butter, milk or cream)

1 large egg

20g (³/4 oz) unsalted butter, melted

¹/2 teaspoon ground cumin

¹/2 teaspoon ground coriander

A pinch of freshly grated nutmeg

Vegetable oil, for deep-frying

Salt and freshly ground black pepper

For the filling:

4 tablespoons olive oil

150g (5oz) lean minced lamb

A good pinch of ground allspice

25g (1oz) unsalted butter

1 small onion, finely chopped

2 tablespoons pine kernels

75g (3oz) feta cheese, crumbled

2 tablespoons chopped mint

---

tip

I LIKE TO SERVE THE KIBBEH with a Middle Eastern-style sauce. Put 150ml (¹/4 pint) plain yoghurt in a saucepan and whisk until smooth. Mix 2 tablespoons of cornflour with a little water to form a paste, add to the yoghurt and stir continually over a low heat until it is just below boiling point and the sauce thickens. Stir in a little crushed garlic and chopped mint and season to taste.

iraqi stuffed potato balls

tip

IF YOU MAKE SMALLER POTATO BALLS, these can be served as a cocktail nibble.

Here simple mashed potato is enlivened with feta cheese, chopped hard-boiled egg, currants and spices, then rolled in shredded raw potato and fried until crisp. Serve with an Arabic-style salad of tomato, cucumber and red onion with a garlic, olive oil and lemon dressing.

Heat the butter in a small pan, add the onion and cook until soft and golden. Add the paprika, allspice and cumin and cook for 1 minute to infuse the onion with the spices. Transfer to a bowl and mix in the feta, hard-boiled egg, chives and currants.

In a separate bowl, mix together the warm mashed potato, cornflour and one of the eggs, then season to taste. Using wet hands, shape into balls the size of golf balls. Make a deep indentation in each one, fill with the feta mixture and then reshape so the filling is completely covered by the potato. Chill for up to 1 hour.

Using the shredding blade of a mandolin (or a grater), shred the baking potatoes and dry in a cloth. Lightly beat the 2 remaining eggs. Remove the potato balls from the fridge, dip them in the beaten egg and then roll them in the shredded potatoes, moulding them with your hand to ensure they are well covered. Heat some vegetable oil to 160°C/325°F in a deep-fat fryer or a deep saucepan. Fry the potato balls in batches in the hot oil for 5–8 minutes, until golden. Remove with a slotted spoon and drain on kitchen paper. Serve.

25g (1oz) unsalted butter

½ onion, finely chopped

¼ teaspoon smoked paprika

¼ teaspoon ground allspice

½ teaspoon ground cumin

200g (7oz) feta cheese, crumbled

1 hard-boiled egg, diced

1 tablespoon chopped chives

2 tablespoons currants, soaked in hot water for 30 minutes and then drained

300g (11oz) warm mashed potato (made without any butter, milk or cream)

1 tablespoon cornflour

3 eggs

2 large baking potatoes, peeled

Vegetable oil, for deep-frying

Salt and freshly ground black pepper

aloo tikki

tip

WITH ITS DISTINCTIVE INDIAN FLAVOUR, the mint chutney goes well with curries, tandoori meats, samosas and much more. Substitute coriander for mint, if preferred.

Put the unpeeled potatoes in a pan, cover with cold water, add a little salt and bring to the boil. Reduce the heat and simmer until tender. Drain and allow to cool slightly, then peel the potatoes and mash well until smooth.

Heat a dry frying pan over a high heat, add the gram flour and toast it for 30 seconds, until lightly coloured. Leave to cool, then add to the mashed potato and season with a little salt. Heat half the ghee or oil in a pan, add the cumin seeds and onion and cook until the onion is golden. Stir in the peas, ginger, green chillies, chilli powder, ground coriander and lemon juice, then add the mashed potatoes, garam masala and fresh coriander. Mix thoroughly, transfer to a bowl and leave to cool.

To make the chutney, simply place all the ingredients in a blender or food processor and blitz to a coarse purée.

Divide the potato mixture into 8 balls, then flatten them to shape into round patties. Heat the remaining ghee or oil in a large frying pan and fry the patties until golden on both sides. Serve with the chutney.

650g (1lb 6oz) floury potatoes

2 tablespoons gram flour (chickpea flour)

4 tablespoons ghee or oil

1 tablespoon cumin seeds

1 onion, finely chopped

150g (5oz) peas, cooked

2.5cm (1in) piece of fresh root ginger, finely chopped

2 green chillies, deseeded and finely chopped

1/2 teaspoon chilli powder

2 teaspoons ground coriander

1 tablespoon lemon juice

1 tablespoon garam masala

1 tablespoon chopped coriander

Salt

For the mint chutney:

1 bunch of mint

2 plum tomatoes, cut into chunks

1 teaspoon cumin seeds

1/2 teaspoon garam masala

1 garlic clove, crushed

Juice of 1/2 lemon

1 teaspoon white wine vinegar

italian potato rissoles

If you asked me what I consider a great marriage of food, tomatoes, mozzarella and basil would surely come to mind. I use it here for topping these delicate potato rissoles. A dish everyone will appreciate.

Place the hot mashed potato in a bowl and beat in half the butter, the egg yolk and some seasoning. Slowly mix in the flour and Parmesan cheese, then the cream, to form a fairly stiff dough. Shape into 8 small, round rissoles.

Heat the oil and the remaining butter in a large frying pan, add the potato rissoles and cook for 4–5 minutes on each side, until golden brown. Transfer to a baking sheet.

For the topping, place a slice of tomato on top of each rissole, then cover with the mozzarella. In a small pan, infuse the olive oil, garlic and basil leaves over a low heat for 1 minute, then spoon them over the rissoles. Season with salt and pepper and place under a hot grill until the cheese just begins to melt.

variation

As an alternative topping, mix 100g (4oz) fromage frais with 1 tablespoon each of chopped chives and dill. Place a dollop on each potato rissole, scatter over 50g (2oz) grated mature Cheddar and place under the grill until hot and bubbling.

125g (4^1/$_2$ oz) hot mashed potato (made without any butter, milk or cream)

50g (2oz) unsalted butter

1 egg yolk

125g (4^1/$_2$ oz) plain flour

50g (2oz) Parmesan cheese, freshly grated

1 tablespoon double cream

2 tablespoons olive oil

Salt and freshly ground black pepper

For the topping:

2 plum tomatoes, skinned and cut into 4 slices each

1 buffalo mozzarella cheese, cut into 8 slices

1 tablespoon olive oil

1 garlic clove, crushed

8 basil leaves

ROtoLO DI patata

*In this recipe, slices of prosciutto replace the usual pasta sheets to
encompass a filling of garlicky porcini mushrooms and mashed potato. A
really flavoursome dish, served with a light balsamic butter.*

Place the unpeeled potatoes in a large pan, cover with water, add a
little salt and bring to the boil. Reduce the heat and simmer until just
tender, then drain well. Peel while still warm and mash until smooth.
Transfer to a bowl and mix in 25g (1oz) of the butter, the egg yolk and
the grated Parmesan.

Heat the oil in a frying pan, add the porcini, shallots and half the garlic
and fry for 2–3 minutes, until the mushrooms are golden and tender.
Add to the mashed potatoes and mix together. Season to taste with
nutmeg, salt and pepper and leave to cool.

Arrange overlapping slices of the prosciutto in a 30cm (12in) square
on a piece of well-buttered foil. Spread the potato mixture over the
prosciutto in a layer about 1cm (½ in) thick. Lifting the foil as you go,
roll it up neatly, making sure the potato mixture is completely covered
by the prosciutto. Refrigerate for 2–3 hours, until the roll is firm.
Carefully remove the foil and cut the roll into 12 slices.

Heat another 25g (1oz) of the butter in a large non-stick frying pan
and fry the slices until golden on both sides. Place in a serving dish
and keep warm. Clean the pan, add the remaining butter and heat
with the remaining garlic and the sage leaves until the butter is
foaming and nutty in fragrance. Stir in the balsamic vinegar. Pour the
foaming butter over the potato slices and top with the Parmesan
shavings. Serve immediately.

450g (1lb) floury potatoes

100g (4oz) unsalted butter

1 egg yolk

**75g (3oz) Parmesan cheese, freshly grated,
plus 50g (2oz) fresh Parmesan shavings,
to serve**

2 tablespoons olive oil

**250g (9oz) fresh porcini mushrooms, thinly
sliced**

2 shallots, finely chopped

1 garlic clove, crushed

Freshly grated nutmeg

250g (9oz) thinly sliced prosciutto

10 small sage leaves

2 tablespoons balsamic vinegar

Salt and freshly ground black pepper

RED WINE-GLAZED POTATO GALETTE WITH SHALLOTS, CHESTNUTS AND LARDONS

Here the potatoes are glazed in red wine, so they not only taste great but also look spectacular. Port works equally well. Serve as an accompaniment to game dishes. For those with a little extra time on their hands, it is well worth making individual portions – they make a stunning presentation.

Preheat the oven to 200°C/400°F/gas mark 6. Heat a dry frying pan until very hot, add the bacon and sauté for 2–3 minutes, until golden and crisp. Stir in the shallots, garlic, chestnuts and parsley, season lightly, then remove from the heat and set aside.

Heat half the duck or goose fat in a 20cm (8in) ovenproof frying pan, then remove from the heat. Arrange half the potatoes in overlapping slices in the pan and season with salt and pepper. Top with the bacon and chestnut mixture, then cover with the remaining potatoes, arranged attractively in overlapping slices. Spoon over the remaining fat and season.

Cook the potatoes on the hob for about 5–8 minutes, until they start to brown underneath. Flip the galette onto a plate, then slide it back into the pan, brown-side uppermost. Continue cooking until the other side is brown. Press down with a plate to compress the potatoes, pour over the wine, then cover with foil and cook for 10 minutes in the oven, pressing the potatoes down occasionally, until the wine has evaporated and the potatoes have taken on a light ruby colour. Turn out onto a serving plate and serve immediately.

75g (3oz) back bacon, cut into lardons (small strips)

4 shallots, thickly sliced

2 large garlic cloves, crushed

75g (3oz) frozen or vacuum-packed chestnuts, (defrosted) and chopped

2 tablespoons chopped parsley

4 tablespoons duck or goose fat

500g (1lb 2oz) waxy potatoes, peeled and cut into slices 3mm ($1/8$ in) thick

100ml ($3^{1}/2$ fl oz) red wine

Salt and freshly ground black pepper

poached egg on potato cheesecakes with portabello mushrooms

This makes a wonderful brunch dish, popular with vegetarians and meat lovers alike. If you add vinegar to the water when poaching eggs, the acid helps to set the protein. Occasionally I vary the cheese in the potato cakes. Creamy Yorkshire Blue or sharp Parmesan make a welcome change.

Place the hot mashed potato in a bowl, add the butter, egg, grated cheese and a little salt and mix together. Gradually knead in the flour, adding enough to bind the mixture to a fairly stiff dough. With floured hands, divide the dough into 4 balls and flatten them into cakes about 9cm (3$\frac{1}{2}$ in) in diameter and 2cm ($\frac{3}{4}$ in) thick. Set aside while you prepare the chive butter.

Bring the water to the boil in a small pan, then whisk in the butter a few pieces at a time to form a light sauce. Season with salt and pepper, add the chives and keep warm.

Fry the potato cakes in the vegetable oil for 2–3 minutes on each side, until golden. Meanwhile, cook the portabello mushrooms under a hot grill for 3–4 minutes on each side, until tender.

To poach the eggs, bring 1 litre (1$\frac{3}{4}$ pints) of water to the boil in a medium pan, add the vinegar, then reduce the heat to just simmering. Swirl the water round with a spoon and carefully crack in the eggs. Cook gently for 2–3 minutes, until the eggs are set but still soft. Carefully remove from the water, using a slotted spoon, and drain on kitchen paper.

Place the potato cakes on serving plates, put a portabello mushroom, rib-side up, on top of each one, then top with a poached egg. Spoon over the chive sauce and serve with crusty bread.

350g (12oz) hot mashed potato (made without any butter, milk or cream)

25g (1oz) unsalted butter

1 small egg, beaten

25g (1oz) mature Cheddar cheese, grated

About 125g (4$\frac{1}{2}$ oz) self-raising flour

4 tablespoons vegetable oil

4 large portabello mushrooms

4 tablespoons vinegar

4 free-range eggs

Salt and freshly ground black pepper

For the chive butter:

5 tablespoons water

125g (4$\frac{1}{2}$ oz) chilled unsalted butter, cut into small pieces

2 tablespoons chopped chives

celeriac and potato trouffade

tip

**GOOD CHEESE SHOPS
and some supermarkets
stock Tomme de Savoie.
If it is unavailable,
cream cheese, although
entirely different,
makes a nice substitute.**

*This classic potato cake from the Auvergne region of France is flavoured
with melting cheese and smoked bacon. I like to include some celeriac, too.*

Heat a 20cm (8in) omelette pan until smoking, add the smoked bacon
and fry until it releases its fat. Add the potatoes and celeriac and cook
for 8–10 minutes, stirring constantly, until they are lightly golden and
starting to soften. Stir in the cheese and parsley, taking care not to
break up the potato and celeriac. Season with salt and pepper. Spread
the mixture level with a palette knife, reduce the heat and cook gently
for 15–20 minutes, until crisp and golden underneath. Turn and cook
the other side, then turn out onto a dish and serve.

100g (4oz) smoked bacon, cut into small
dice

250g (9oz) waxy potatoes, peeled and cut
into 1cm (^{1}/2 in) cubes

125g (4^1/2 oz) celeriac, peeled and cut into
1cm (^{1}/2 in) cubes

150g (5oz) Tomme de Savoie cheese, diced

2 tablespoons chopped parsley

Salt and freshly ground black pepper

perfect fries

4 large, floury potatoes
Sunflower oil or lard, for deep-frying
Coarse sea salt

Peel the potatoes, rinse under cold water and then dry on kitchen paper. Cut them into strips about 1cm ($^1/_2$ in) wide by 5–7.5cm (2–3in) long.

Half-fill a deep-fat fryer or deep, heavy-based pan with sunflower oil or lard and heat it to 150°C/300°F. Fry the potatoes in the oil in batches for 5–8 minutes, until they are soft but still very pale. Lift out and drain on kitchen paper (the chips can be prepared up to this stage several hours in advance, as long as the final frying is done just before serving).

Raise the temperature of the oil to 200°C/400°F and return the chips, in batches again, to the pan. Fry for 2–3 minutes, until golden and crisp. Drain on kitchen paper and pile onto a hot serving plate. Sprinkle liberally with coarse sea salt and serve.

CHIPS TO BRAG ABOUT

DIPS FOR CHIPS AND FRIES

Here are my favourite dips for serving with chips:

- Mustard-smoked paprika mayo (see page 139).
- Harissa mayonnaise – simply stir harissa paste into good-quality mayonnaise until it is spicy enough for your taste.
- Tomato and fresh ginger mayonnaise – finely grate a 1cm ($^1/_2$ in) piece of fresh root ginger and stir it into 100ml ($3^1/_2$ fl oz) good-quality mayonnaise with tomato ketchup to taste.

BARBECUE FRENCH FRIES

You won't need all the barbecue spice mix for this recipe but the rest can be stored in an airtight container for about a month. It is very adaptable and can be sprinkled over vegetables or rubbed on fish or meat before barbecuing or grilling.

4 large, floury potatoes

Sunflower oil, for deep-frying

Sea salt

For the barbecue spice mix:

2 tablespoons dried red chilli flakes

1$^1/_2$ tablespoons paprika

1$^1/_2$ teaspoons ground cumin

1$^1/_2$ teaspoons ground coriander

1$^1/_2$ teaspoons caster sugar

1 teaspoon salt

$^1/_2$ teaspoon mustard powder

$^1/_2$ teaspoon freshly ground black pepper

$^1/_2$ teaspoon dried thyme

$^1/_2$ teaspoon mild curry powder

1 teaspoon cayenne pepper

For the barbecue spice mix, put all the ingredients in a bowl and mix until thoroughly combined.

Prepare and cook the chips as for the Perfect Fries (see page 106). After the second frying, place them in a baking tin lined with kitchen paper to absorb excess oil, season lightly with sea salt, then sprinkle with about 2 tablespoons of the barbecue spice mix. Serve immediately.

OVEN CHIPS

Okay, so you can buy oven chips in the supermarket but really, should you? This is an easy alternative to chips, with no pans full of deep fat needing constant attention. All you need is a large baking tin.

650g (1lb 6oz) floury potatoes

4 tablespoons vegetable oil

Sea salt and freshly ground black pepper

Preheat the oven to 200°C/400°F/gas mark 6. Cut the unpeeled potatoes into thick wedges and lay them flat in a single layer in a large baking tin. Pour over the oil and toss with the potatoes, then season with coarse sea salt and a little pepper. Place in the oven and cook for 30 minutes, by which time they should have coloured on the base. Turn them over and continue cooking for 10–15 minutes, until they are golden and wonderfully crisp. Serve hot from the oven.

VARIATION

Orange- or white-fleshed sweet potatoes, used in exactly the same way, also make great chips.

if you think the recipes in this chapter will err on the stodgy side you are in for a pleasant surprise. Potatoes can add lightness to many dishes, especially breads, pancakes and pies. Some of the pies are hearty affairs, such as the Potato, Mozzarella and Salami Pie (page 131), but others are delicate little morsels that can even be served as canapés: try the Smoked Ham and Roquefort Kipfel (page 124) or the Potato and Salt Cod Empanadas (page 125).

Originally, adding potato to the dough when making bread was a way of making precious flour go further, but potato breads soon became prized for their light texture and good keeping qualities. Potato breads are common in many different cuisines, from the Farls and Boxty of Ireland (pages 114 and 111) to the Potato Pooris of India (page 115) and the Lefse, or flat bread, of Norway (page 117).

Potato pancakes are hugely popular throughout the world and sadly there is only room for a small selection in this chapter. They can be surprisingly sophisticated – for the ultimate light and fluffy potato pancake, try the famous Crêpes Vonnasienne on page 121, from Georges Blanc's legendary restaurant in France.

BREADS, PANCAKES AND PIES

Basic potato Bread

This versatile bread has good keeping qualities and can be used as you would any white loaf. I like it as a base for Welsh rarebit and also use it to make Cuban Bread Pudding (see page 166).

Warm the oven to 125°C/240°F/gas mark ¹/2. Put the yeast, half the sugar and a little of the milk in a small bowl and mix until dissolved. Put the flour in a bowl and warm briefly in the oven. Rub in the butter, then stir in the remaining sugar, the warm mashed potato and the salt. Pour in the remaining milk, the yeast mixture and the beaten egg and mix to a soft, pliable dough, adding a little water if necessary. Turn out onto a lightly floured work surface and knead thoroughly for 8–10 minutes, then place in a clean bowl, cover with a cloth and leave in a warm place for about 45 minutes or until doubled in volume.

Knock back the risen dough with floured hands, turn it out onto a floured surface and knead for a couple of minutes. Shape into a round loaf and place on a greased baking sheet. Cover and leave to rise again for about 30 minutes or until doubled in size.

Preheat the oven to 200°C/400°F/gas mark 6. Brush the loaf with a little beaten egg and bake for 25–30 minutes, until it is well-browned and sounds hollow when tapped underneath. Transfer to a wire rack and leave to cool.

25g (1oz) fresh yeast

40g (1¹/2 oz) caster sugar

150ml (¹/4 pint) lukewarm full-fat milk

450g (1lb) strong white flour

50g (2oz) unsalted butter, cut into small pieces

100g (4oz) warm mashed potato (made without any butter, milk or cream)

1 teaspoon salt

1 egg, beaten, plus a little extra beaten egg to glaze

boxty bread

I found this recipe in an old cookery book when travelling through Ireland. Boxty is a traditional Irish potato dish, created at a time when wheat flour was an expensive commodity so potatoes became a cheaper alternative. It can be prepared as a scone-like bread, as below, or thinned with milk and cooked as a pancake on a griddle. Both methods are delicious.

225g (8oz) large, floury potatoes, peeled and coarsely grated

225g (8oz) mashed potato (made without any butter, milk or cream)

175g (6oz) plain flour

1 teaspoon baking powder

50g (2oz) unsalted butter, softened

1/2 teaspoon salt

Preheat the oven to 180°C/350°F/gas mark 4. Place the grated potatoes in a thin tea towel or a piece of muslin and squeeze out all the liquid. Place in a bowl, add the mashed potatoes, flour, baking powder, softened butter and salt and mix well.

Turn the mixture out onto a floured board and divide in half. Roll each portion into a round about 5mm (1/4in) thick and score a cross on the top. Place on a well-buttered baking sheet and bake for about 40 minutes, until browned and risen. Serve hot from the oven, broken into quarters, with lashings of butter.

fennel seed and sweet potato bread

A recipe I've had in my possession for many years. I don't know where it originates from but it's an excellent bread.

Preheat the oven to 190°C/375°F/gas mark 5. Put the sweet potato in a roasting tin and bake for about 1 hour or until soft. Peel the potato, discarding the skin, sieve the flesh and set aside to cool.

Sift the flour and salt into a large bowl and rub in the butter until the mixture resembles breadcrumbs. Cream the yeast and sugar together and mix in 215ml (7^1/$_2$ fl oz) of the milk and the beaten eggs. Make a well in the centre of the flour and add the sweet potato, followed by the yeasty liquid. Using first a knife, then one hand, mix to a soft dough, adding more milk if necessary. Turn out onto a lightly floured surface and knead for about 10 minutes, until the dough is smooth and elastic. Put into a clean bowl, cover with clingfilm and leave to rise in a warm place for about 1 hour or until it is one and a half times its original size. Turn out onto a floured board, sprinkle on the coriander, fennel and pumpkin seeds and knead for 5 minutes. Shape the loaf into a round and place on an oiled baking sheet. Make some cuts across the top, cover with oiled clingfilm and leave in a warm place for 15 minutes or until it has increased by one and a half times its size.

Preheat the oven to 200°C/400°F/gas mark 6. Carefully brush the top of the loaf with egg glaze and bake for 35–40 minutes, until it is well-risen and sounds hollow when turned out of the tin and tapped underneath.

1 large sweet potato, weighing about 225–275g (8–10oz)

675g (1^1/$_2$ lb) strong white flour

1 tablespoon salt

55g (2oz) unsalted butter, cut into small pieces

25g (1oz) fresh yeast

2 teaspoons caster sugar

About 300ml (^{1}/$_2$ pint) lukewarm milk

2 eggs, beaten, plus a little extra beaten egg to glaze

3 tablespoons fennel seeds, toasted briefly in a dry frying pan

25g (1oz) pumpkin seeds

2 teaspoons ground coriander

potato farls

Serve these traditional Irish farls with butter and sugar or jam, or with Ulster fry (see below).

250g (9oz) floury potatoes, peeled and cut into chunks

25g (1oz) unsalted butter, melted

50g (2oz) plain flour

A pinch of salt

tip

FARLS ARE BEST MADE while the potatoes are hot. If they cool down, reheat in the microwave for about 30 seconds. If you prefer, cut the rolled-out dough into individual rounds (5cm/2in).

Put the potatoes in a pan, cover with cold water, add a little salt and bring to the boil. Simmer until tender, then drain well and return to the pan to dry over a low heat. Mash until smooth, place in a bowl and beat in the melted butter. Stir in the flour and salt to make a fairly soft, pliable dough. Turn out onto a lightly floured surface and roll out into a 20–23cm (8–9in) round, about 5mm (1/4 in) thick. Cut into 6 wedges (farls) and cook in a hot, heavy-based frying pan or on a flat cast-iron griddle, without any fat, for about 2 minutes on each side, until lightly browned. Serve hot.

ulster fry

Take pork sausages, bacon, black pudding, tomatoes and eggs and prepare a traditional fried breakfast. The eggs are best fried in the fat after cooking the bacon. Serve hot with the potato farls. A slice of caramelised apple is also good with this breakfast, although not truly traditional.

potato POORIS

tip

TO MAKE GARAM MASALA, mix together 4 teaspoons ground cardamom, 1 teaspoon ground cinnamon, ½ teaspoon ground cloves, 1 teaspoon ground cumin and 1 teaspoon ground black pepper. Store in an airtight container.

Pooris are eaten for breakfast in northern India, usually as an accompaniment to a potato-based dish. This recipe includes potato in the dough. They make an ideal accompaniment to a traditional-style thali.

Bake the potato until tender (see page 70), then peel while hot and push the flesh through a sieve into a bowl. Briefly toast the cardamom, caraway and cumin seeds in a hot dry frying pan until aromatic and lightly coloured, then stir them into the potato.

Sift the flour into a bowl and stir in the ground cumin, black pepper, garam masala, chopped coriander, chilli and some salt. Add the potato and, using your fingertips, mix into the flour. Add the oil and knead to form a dough, adding a little warm water if the dough is too firm. Turn out onto a lightly floured surface and knead for 8–10 minutes, until smooth and elastic, then shape into a smooth ball. Put the dough back in the bowl, coat it with a little oil, cover with a damp tea towel and leave to rest for 45 minutes.

Turn out the dough and knead for 2–3 minutes, then divide into 8 balls. Flatten each one with the palm of your hand and then roll out on a floured surface into a 20cm (8in) round. Heat some oil in a deep-fat fryer or a deep saucepan to 160°C/325°F. Fry the pooris until golden, turning them occasionally in the oil and pushing them under with a wooden spoon or fish slice to keep them submerged. Drain on kitchen paper and keep warm until all the pooris are cooked.

1 large baking potato

½ teaspoon cardamom seeds

½ teaspoon caraway seeds

1 teaspoon cumin seeds

150g (5oz) strong white flour

½ teaspoon ground cumin

¼ teaspoon cracked black pepper

1 teaspoon garam masala (see Tip)

1 tablespoon chopped coriander

1 green chilli, deseeded and chopped

2 tablespoons vegetable oil

Oil, for deep-frying

Salt

ROLLeD italian potato BReaD

This stuffed bread is packed full of sunny Italian flavours. It makes great picnic food. Left unrolled, it can be cooked like a pizza.

Mix the yeast with the warm water. Sift the flour and salt into a bowl and stir in the mashed potato. Make a well in the centre, add the yeast liquid and mix to make a fairly soft dough. Turn out onto a floured surface and knead for about 10 minutes, until smooth and pliable. Place in a clean bowl, cover with a cloth and leave in a warm place for 1–1¹/₂ hours, until doubled in size.

Knock back the risen dough and roll out to a 30 x 25cm (12 x 10in) rectangle, about 5mm (¹/4 in) thick. Arrange the new potato slices over the dough leaving a border of about 2.5cm (1in) all the way round. Top the potatoes with the prosciutto, scatter over the mozzarella and basil, then drizzle over half the olive oil. Season with salt and pepper. Roll up the dough to secure the filling, drizzle over the remaining olive oil and place on a greased baking sheet. Cover and leave in a warm place for about 40 minutes, until risen. Meanwhile, preheat the oven to 180°C/350°F/gas mark 4. Bake the bread for 30–35 minutes, until golden. Leave to cool before serving.

25g (1oz) fresh yeast

350ml (12fl oz) lukewarm water

400g (14oz) strong white flour

1 teaspoon salt

150g (5oz) mashed potato (made without any butter, milk or cream)

For the filling:

250g (9oz) cooked new potatoes, sliced

150g (5oz) thinly sliced prosciutto

150g (5oz) mozzarella cheese, diced

10 basil leaves

4 tablespoons olive oil

Coarse salt and freshly ground black pepper

Lefse potato fLat BREAD

This recipe comes from Norway, where it is generally prepared on festive occasions. A special grid-like rolling pin called a lefse is used, but your good old rolling pin at home will do fine. I like to serve these flat breads wrapped around some smoked salmon and a little creamed horseradish.

900g (2lb) baking potatoes

25g (1oz) unsalted butter

225g (8oz) self-raising flour

Coarse salt and freshly ground black pepper

Bake the potatoes until tender (see page 70), then cut them in half, scoop out the flesh and pass it through a sieve or a potato ricer. Mix in the butter and a little seasoning and leave to cool. Stir in 175g (6oz) of the flour, then gradually add the remaining flour to make a stiff dough (you may not need all the flour). Divide the dough into 4, then divide each portion into 4 again. On a floured surface, roll out each piece to a paper-thin disc.

Heat a flat cast-iron griddle or a large, non-stick frying pan until fairly hot and cook each disc for 1–2 minutes on each side, until patched with brown. Stack them on top of each other as you remove them from the pan, to keep them warm and soft.

pear and potato rösti with black pudding and raclette

These are not really traditional rösti but are more like a cross between rösti and latkes – the difference being that rösti are made simply with grated potato but these include some potato flour to soak up the moisture from the pear and help bind the mixture. They are topped with black pudding and slices of raclette, an exceptionally good melting cheese from Valais in Switzerland and the Savoie region of France.

Cook the potatoes in their skins in boiling salted water until not quite done, then drain well in a colander. Peel the potatoes and leave to cool. Grate them coarsely, place them in a clean tea towel and squeeze out as much liquid as possible. Place the grated potato in a bowl.

Peel, core and grate the pear, then squeeze out the moisture from it in the same way. Add to the potatoes and season to taste, then stir in the egg yolk and potato flour. Heat a frying pan until very hot, add the bacon and fry until crisp. Add to the potato mixture and mix well.

Heat half the vegetable oil in a heavy-based frying pan and place 8 buttered 7.5cm (3in) metal rings in it (or use 4 at a time, depending on the size of your pan). Spoon the potato mixture into the rings so it is about 1cm (^{1}/2 in) thick and cook for about 10 minutes on each side, until brown and crisp, pressing down from time to time. Remove from the pan and keep warm. Heat the remaining oil in the pan and fry the slices of black pudding until crisp and browned on each side.

Place three slices of black pudding on each rösti, top with a slice of raclette and place under a hot grill until melted. Serve immediately.

450g (1lb) waxy potatoes

1 ripe but firm pear

1 egg yolk

2 tablespoons potato flour (or arrowroot)

75g (3oz) smoked streaky bacon, chopped

4 tablespoons vegetable oil

24 small slices of best-quality black pudding

8 slices of raclette cheese

Salt and freshly ground black pepper

tip

RACLETTE CHEESE and potatoes is a traditional combination in Switzerland. For a simple but luxurious treat, just melt a generous quantity of raclette in a pan, then pour it immediately over a dish of hot boiled new potatoes and serve with pickles.

potato socca with chicken livers à la provençale

Socca are baked chickpea pancakes, sold by street vendors in the south of France. They are tasty and easy to make. Here I have added grated potato to the basic chickpea flour batter.

Preheat the oven to 240°C/475°F/gas mark 9. For the socca, cook the potatoes in a pan of boiling salted water until just tender, then drain and peel. Grate the potatoes and set aside. Put the chickpea flour in a bowl and add the water in a steady stream, whisking constantly, to create a smooth batter. Add the olive oil and season with salt and pepper. Stir in the grated potatoes.

Pour a thin layer of olive oil into a large, heavy baking tin and place in the oven until almost smoking. Pour the batter into the tin – it should be about 2.5cm (1in) deep – and place in the oven. Immediately turn the oven off and place the baking tin under a very hot grill. This gives extra heat to the top of the socca, while still retaining the all-round warmth of the oven. Cook for about 10–15 minutes, pricking any bubbles with the point of a knife as they form, until the socca is browned on top and even lightly charred in places. It should be set underneath but still soft and moist. Keep warm while you make the filling.

Heat the olive oil in a frying pan until smoking. Add the chicken livers and cook for about 3–4 minutes, until browned on the outside but still pink in the centre. Remove from the pan and keep warm. Add the garlic, shallots and butter to the pan and cook until the shallots are just tender. Pour in the white wine and simmer until reduced by half, then add the tomatoes, honey and olives and heat through gently. Return the chicken livers to the pan with the basil leaves and some seasoning and reheat briefly.

2 tablespoons olive oil

225g (8oz) chicken livers

2 garlic cloves, crushed

2 shallots, diced

25g (1oz) unsalted butter

4 tablespoons dry white wine

100g (4oz) sun-blush tomatoes

1 tablespoon runny honey

12 black olives

6 basil leaves

Salt and freshly ground black pepper

For the socca:

175g (6oz) waxy potatoes

125g (4¹/₂ oz) chickpea flour (gram flour)

375ml (13fl oz) water

2 tablespoons olive oil, plus extra for cooking

crêpes vonnasienne

tip

SERVE THE
PANCAKES topped
with smoked
salmon, caviar and
crème fraîche or, one
of my favourites,
thinly sliced
carpaccio of haddock
with herb mustard
crème fraîche.

These fluffy potato pancakes are the signature dish of the world-renowned restaurant, La Mère Blanc, in Vonnas, near Lyons.

Place the potatoes in a pan, cover with cold water, add some salt and bring to the boil. Cover and simmer until tender, then drain in a colander and return the potatoes to the pan. Add the milk and mash well, making sure there aren't any lumps. Whisk in the potato flour, then whisk in the whole eggs one at a time, followed by the egg whites. Add the cream and season to taste. Leave to rest for 20 minutes before use but do not refrigerate.

Heat a very thin layer of clarified butter in a non-stick frying pan and drop in about 2 tablespoons of batter at a time to make little pancakes about 5mm (1/4 in) thick and 7.5cm (3in) in diameter. Cook for 1–2 minutes, until golden and slightly crisp underneath, then flip over and cook for 2 minutes longer. Remove from the pan and drain on kitchen paper. Serve hot.

250g (9oz) floury potatoes, peeled and cut
   into chunks
100ml (3 1/2 fl oz) full-fat milk
2 tablespoons potato flour (or plain flour)
2 eggs
2 egg whites
4 tablespoons double cream
Clarified butter, for frying (see Tip on
   page 153)
Salt and freshly ground black pepper

stacked potato blintzes with bacon and bananas

Here's a wonderful breakfast dish featuring the unusual combination of crisp bacon and sweet bananas.

For the blintzes, mix together the warm mashed potato and flour, then stir in the egg and egg yolk. Gradually add enough milk to make a batter that drops easily off the spoon. Season with salt and pepper. Heat the butter in a non-stick frying pan and drop in about 2 tablespoons of batter at a time to make little pancakes about 5mm (1/4 in) thick and 7.5cm (3in) in diameter (you will need 8 pancakes altogether). Cook for 2–3 minutes on each side, until golden and set, then remove from the pan and keep warm.

Peel and quarter the bananas. Heat the butter and sugar in a frying pan until lightly caramelised, then add the bananas and cook until golden. Meanwhile, fry or grill the bacon until crisp. Put half the pancakes on 4 serving plates and cover with the caramelised bananas. Top with the remaining pancakes, then the bacon. Pour over the maple syrup and serve immediately.

2 large bananas

25g (1oz) unsalted butter

1 tablespoon brown sugar

8 streaky bacon rashers, rind removed

100ml (3^1/$_2$ fl oz) maple syrup

For the blintzes:

175g (6oz) warm mashed potato (made without any butter, milk or cream)

75g (3oz) plain flour

1 egg

1 egg yolk

About 100ml (3^1/$_2$ fl oz) full-fat milk

25g (1oz) unsalted butter

Salt and freshly ground black pepper

smoked ham and roquefort kipfel

Kipfel is a type of savoury Austrian croissant, filled with all manner of interesting things. I've added some potato to the dough, which acts as a great base for the ham and cheese filling. Quark cheese is often used in both the dough and the filling but I like to add the salty tang of blue cheese, which I feel gives a better flavour.

To make the dough, put the potato in a pan, cover with cold water, add some salt and bring to the boil. Cover and simmer for 10 minutes, then drain and leave to cool. Peel the potato and grate finely.

In a bowl, mix together the quark, flour, butter, egg, nutmeg and salt, then stir in the grated potato to make a pliable dough. Cover and leave to relax for up to 1 hour.

Meanwhile, prepare the filling. Melt the butter in a pan, stir in the flour and cook over a low heat for 1 minute. Beat in the cream with a wooden spoon and simmer for a minute or two to make a very thick sauce. Remove from the heat and leave until lukewarm. Stir in the herbs, ham and Roquefort and chill thoroughly.

Preheat the oven to 220°C/425°F/gas mark 7. On a lightly floured surface, roll the dough out into a long rectangle, 12cm (5in) wide, and then cut it into triangles measuring about 12cm (5in) on each side. Divide the filling between the triangles and roll up into croissants so the filling is completely enclosed. Place on a baking tray and brush with the egg and milk glaze. Bake for 25–30 minutes, until golden brown and delicious!

¹/2 tablespoon unsalted butter

¹/2 tablespoon plain flour

100ml (3¹/2 fl oz) double cream

1 tablespoon chopped marjoram

1 tablespoon chopped parsley

150g (5oz) cooked smoked ham, chopped

75g (3oz) Roquefort cheese, chilled and cut into 1cm (¹/2 in) dice

A little beaten egg and milk, to glaze

For the dough:

1 small floury potato, weighing about 100g (4oz)

100g (4oz) quark (or cream cheese)

100g (4oz) plain flour

50g (2oz) unsalted butter, softened

1 egg

Freshly grated nutmeg, to taste

Salt

potato and salt cod empanadas with orange and red pepper relish

First make the relish. Grate the zest from one of the oranges, then peel and segment both of them. Chop the segments, reserving the juice. Place the chopped orange, sun-dried tomatoes, roasted peppers and garlic in a bowl and stir in the orange juice and zest. Put the sugar and vinegar in a pan and boil for 2 minutes, then pour over the orange and red pepper mixture. Leave to cool.

To make the salt cod, put the cod in a small dish, cover with the sea salt and leave for 2 hours. Wash the salt from the fish by running it under cold water, then put it in a pan with the milk, garlic and potatoes and poach until the cod and potatoes are tender. Remove the fish and potatoes from the cooking liquid with a slotted spoon. Mash them together, then stir in the olive oil and enough of the milk to give a fairly firm consistency, like stiff mashed potato. Season with salt, pepper and cayenne and stir in the parsley. Leave to cool, then chill.

For the pastry, sift the flour and salt into a bowl and rub in the butter with your fingertips until the mixture resembles fine breadcrumbs. Pour in the water and bring the dough together into a ball. Cover with clingfilm and leave to rest in the fridge for 1 hour.

Preheat the oven to 200°C/400°F/gas mark 6. Roll out the dough on a lightly floured surface until it is about 3mm ($1/8$ in) thick. Cut out twelve 10cm (4in) rounds and place a good spoonful of the salt cod mixture in the centre of each one. Fold the pastry in half to form a semi-circle, pressing the edges firmly together. Crimp the edges with your fingers to seal, so they look like little Cornish pasties. Place the empanadas on a baking sheet, brush with the beaten egg, then bake for 10–15 minutes, until golden brown. Serve hot, with the orange and red pepper relish.

200g (7oz) fresh cod fillet, without skin

50g (2oz) sea salt

200ml (7fl oz) full-fat milk

3 garlic cloves, crushed

300g (11oz) waxy potatoes, peeled and cut into 5mm ($1/4$ in) dice

3 tablespoons olive oil

A pinch of cayenne pepper

3 tablespoons chopped parsley

Salt and freshly ground black pepper

For the relish:

2 oranges

6 sun-dried tomatoes, chopped

4 red peppers, roasted, skinned, deseeded and chopped

1 garlic clove, crushed

2 tablespoons caster sugar

4 tablespoons balsamic vinegar

For the pastry:

500g (1lb 2oz) plain flour

A pinch of salt

150g (5oz) unsalted butter, cut into small pieces

100ml ($3^1/2$ fl oz) water

A little beaten egg, to glaze

scamorza, ricotta and spinach knishes

You could describe knishes as the Jewish answer to the spring roll. They are usually filled with meat, potatoes, cheese or chicken livers and are served on Jewish festival days as a starter or canapé. Scamorza is an Italian cheese, usually smoked, and is rather like a cross between mozzarella and provolone. If you cannot find it, use provolone instead.

250g (9oz) floury potatoes, peeled and cut into chunks

6 spring onions, chopped

75g (3oz) unsalted butter

125g (4 1/2 oz) ricotta cheese, drained (see Tip)

125g (4 1/2 oz) fresh spinach, cooked and roughly chopped

75g (3oz) scamorza cheese, thinly shaved

3 tablespoons raisins, soaked in hot water for 30 minutes, then well-drained

A few fresh white breadcrumbs (see Tip on page 86)

3 large sheets of filo pastry

Salt and freshly ground black pepper

Put the potatoes in a pan, cover with cold water, add some salt and bring to the boil. Reduce the heat and simmer until just tender, then drain in a colander. Return the potatoes to the pan and dry out over a low heat. Place in a large bowl and mash well. Add the spring onions, 25g (1oz) of the butter, the drained ricotta and the chopped spinach. Season to taste. Stir in the scamorza and soaked raisins, then add enough breadcrumbs to firm up the mixture. Leave to cool.

Preheat the oven to 190°C/375°F/gas mark 5. Melt the remaining butter in a pan. Lay out one sheet of filo pastry on a work surface and brush with melted butter. Top with a second sheet and brush with butter again, then top with the final sheet of filo. Cut the stack of filo into 4 horizontal sections, then cut lengthways in half to give 8 sections. Place 2–3 tablespoons of the potato mixture on each filo section, fold in the sides and roll up like spring rolls. Brush with the remaining melted butter and place on a lightly greased baking sheet. Bake in the oven for 10–12 minutes, until golden and crisp.

tip

TO DRAIN RICOTTA CHEESE, line a colander with muslin or thin cloth and place it over a bowl. Put the ricotta in the colander, draw up the muslin round it and tie into a bundle with string. Leave overnight in a cool place to drain off excess liquid.

rustic potato, yorkshire blue and walnut tarts

Serves 6

Heat the olive oil in a pan, add the onion and thyme and cook for 8–10 minutes until the onion is lightly coloured. Cook the potatoes in boiling salted water for 5–8 minutes, until just tender, then drain in a colander.

Put the onion, fresh thyme, potatoes, chives, cheese, walnuts and crème fraîche in a bowl and season to taste. Place in the refrigerator until needed.

Preheat the oven to 200°C/400°F/gas mark 6. Lay the pastry out flat on a work surface and cut it into 6 rectangles; it should be fairly thin, so if necessary roll it out a little more first. Place the rectangles on a baking sheet and divide the filling between them, leaving a 1cm (1/2 in) border. Score the border with a criss-cross pattern and knock up the edges with the back of a knife. Bake the tarts for 20–25 minutes, until the pastry is golden brown.

2 tablespoons olive oil

1 onion, thinly sliced

1 teaspoon thyme leaves

350g (12oz) small waxy potatoes, thinly sliced (but not peeled)

1 tablespoon chopped chives

200g (7oz) Yorkshire Blue cheese, cut into 1cm (1/2 in) dice

2 tablespoons chopped walnuts

2 tablespoons crème fraîche

375g (13oz) ready-rolled puff pastry

Salt and freshly ground black pepper

potato, leek and mustard torte

This tart has a potato and leek filling in a light cream. It is delicious, and very simple to prepare. I like to serve it with a crisp frisée salad with a hazelnut oil dressing.

Divide the puff pastry in half and roll out each piece into a 25cm (10in) circle. Place on a baking sheet, prick with a fork and chill until firm.

Cook the potatoes in their skins in a pan of boiling salted water until tender, then drain well and leave until cool enough to handle. Peel the potatoes and cut them into slices 1cm (1/2 in) thick.

Heat the butter and oil in a pan, add the leeks and cook gently for 4–5 minutes, until tender. Stir in the crème fraîche, thyme, mustard and nutmeg and season to taste.

Preheat the oven to 200°C/400°F/gas mark 6. Arrange a third of the potato slices on one of the pastry circles, leaving a 2.5cm (1in) border all round. Place half the leek mixture on top of the potatoes, then another layer of potatoes, the remaining leek mixture and finally the remaining potatoes. Top with the second pastry circle and press lightly together. Using a very sharp knife, make vertical cuts along the pastry edges and then decorate the top by making cuts radiating in an arc shape from the centre. Brush with beaten egg and milk and bake for 35–40 minutes, until golden.

450g (1lb) puff pastry

200g (7oz) waxy potatoes

15g (1/2 oz) unsalted butter

1 tablespoon vegetable oil

150g (5oz) small leeks, sliced

2 tablespoons crème fraîche

1 teaspoon thyme leaves

2 teaspoons Dijon mustard

1/2 teaspoon freshly grated nutmeg

A little beaten egg and milk, to glaze

Salt and freshly ground black pepper

potato, mozzarella and salami pie

Cook the potatoes in their skins in boiling salted water until just tender, then drain and leave to cool. Peel the potatoes and cut them into slices 5mm (1/4 in) thick. Set aside.

Preheat the oven to 200°C/400°F/gas mark 6. Lightly grease an 18–20cm (7–8in) springform cake tin with a little of the melted butter. Line the tin with filo, letting it overhang the sides, and brush with melted butter. Add another layer of filo and brush with more melted butter. Repeat until all the filo has been used up.

Season the cooked potatoes well and arrange half of them in overlapping slices in the base of the dish. Sprinkle over half the chopped parsley, then half the salami, in overlapping slices, followed by half the mozzarella. Cover with the sliced eggs. Spread over the crème fraîche, then sprinkle over a teaspoon of water. Add another layer of salami, then the mozzarella, sprinkle over the remaining parsley, then add a final layer of potatoes, seasoning as you go. Fold the overhanging filo pastry over the filling and brush with the remaining melted butter.

Bake for 20–25 minutes or until the pastry is golden brown and crisp. Leave the pie to cool slightly in the tin before turning it out onto a board. Cut into thick slices and serve hot or at room temperature. Both are equally delicious!

600g (1lb 5oz) large new potatoes, preferably Charlotte

50g (2oz) unsalted butter, melted

12 sheets of filo pastry

2 tablespoons roughly chopped flat-leaf parsley

100g (4oz) salami, thinly sliced

1 buffalo mozzarella cheese, thinly sliced

5 eggs, hard-boiled and thinly sliced

100ml (3 1/2 fl oz) crème fraîche

Salt and freshly ground black pepper

steak, kidney and mushroom pie in potato pastry

I have used a flaky potato pastry to top this classic British pie. Parsnip, Potato and Honey Mustard Mash (see page 47) makes an ideal accompaniment.

To make the pastry, mix the flour and potatoes together, then rub in 100g (4oz) of the butter. Stir in the iced water and bring together into a dough. Place in a bowl, cover with a cloth and leave to rest for 30 minutes. Roll out the pastry into a 15 x 20cm (6 x 8in) rectangle, about 5mm (1/4 in) thick. Dot half the remaining butter over two-thirds of it, then fold up the unbuttered third, followed by the top third. Press the edges together to seal, turn the pastry 90 degrees and roll out into a rectangle again. Dot with the remaining butter, then fold, turn the pastry and roll out as before. Cover and leave in the fridge for about 2 hours.

Meanwhile, make the filling. Preheat the oven to 160°C/325°F/gas mark 3. Season the beef and kidneys. Heat the oil in a large, heavy-based casserole until very hot and seal the beef in batches (don't overcrowd the pan) until browned all over. Seal the kidneys too, then transfer the beef and kidneys to separate plates. Melt the butter in the same pan, add the onion and fry until golden. Return the beef to the pan, add the Worcestershire sauce and cook for 2–3 minutes. Stir in the tomato purée and mix well, then rain in the flour and cook for 3–4 minutes. Pour in the stout and stock and bring to the boil, stirring constantly, to make a sauce. Reduce the heat, cover the pan with a lid and transfer to the oven. Cook for up to 2 hours, until the meat is tender, adding the mushrooms and kidneys about 15 minutes before the meat is ready. Adjust the seasoning and put the mixture in a large pie dish (or divide it between 4 individual pie dishes).

Roll out the pastry on a lightly floured surface until it is 3mm (1/8 in) thick and use to cover the pie dish. Brush with beaten egg, then place in an oven preheated to 190°C/375°F/gas mark 5 and cook for 30–35 minutes until golden. Leave to cool slightly before serving.

750g (1lb 10oz) topside or chuck steak, cut into 2.5cm (1in) cubes

250g (9oz) veal kidneys, cut into 2.5cm (1in) cubes

4 tablespoons vegetable oil

50g (2oz) unsalted butter

1 onion, finely chopped

4 tablespoons Worcestershire sauce

2 tablespoons tomato purée

50g (2oz) plain flour

300ml (1/2 pint) stout

750ml (1 1/4 pints) beef stock

250g (9oz) button mushrooms, halved

A little beaten egg, to glaze

Salt and freshly ground black pepper

For the potato pastry:

150g (5oz) self-raising flour

100g (4oz) mashed potato (made without any milk, butter or cream), at room temperature

150g (5oz) unsalted butter, cut into small pieces

5 tablespoons iced water

pLenty of

pLenty of other dishes in this book can be served as main courses but the ones in this chapter defy categorisation by cooking method and some take a little extra time and effort to prepare. Many of them can be multiplied easily to serve large numbers, particularly the more homely 'supper' dishes, such as Brixham Fish Pie (page 141), Irish Stew (page 153), My Favourite Cottage Pie (page 152) and Lamb and Potato Hotpot (page 155). Recipes such as these, if we take the trouble to prepare them properly, are fit for any gathering.

Other dishes in this chapter are more recognisably for 'special occasions', demonstrating that potatoes make a perfect partner for luxurious ingredients. Try them in a creamy sauce with John Dory, morels, leeks and truffles (page 137); as a fennel-scented crust for sea bass (page 140), or a replacement for rice in a risotto served with roast turbot (page 144).

Finally, potatoes really come into their own as vegetarian main courses. There are three included in this chapter, but vegetarians will find many more ideas throughout the book.

main COURSES

mackerel plaki with saffron potatoes, lemon and tomato

Plaki is an easy-going Greek dish of fish and vegetables baked together in the oven. I like to make it with mackerel, which I consider one of the most underrated of the cheaper fish. It's appreciated more in Europe than in Britain, which is a great shame, as it has a wonderful flavour and moist texture and is full of nutrients.

Preheat the oven to 180°C/350°F/gas mark 4. Heat 4 tablespoons of the olive oil in a frying pan, add the onion and garlic and cook until softened. Stir in half the thyme and oregano, plus the tomatoes and olives. Then add the sliced potatoes, sprinkle over the saffron and add just enough water to cover. Cook gently for 5–10 minutes, until the potatoes are just tender.

Grease a large ovenproof dish with the remaining oil. Season the fish inside and out and put them in the dish. Sprinkle over the remaining thyme and oregano and spread the potato mixture on top. Pour over the white wine, lemon juice and zest, then bake, uncovered, for 20–25 minutes, until the mackerel are cooked.

6 tablespoons olive oil

1 small red onion, cut into rings

3 garlic cloves, crushed

1/2 teaspoon thyme leaves

1/2 teaspoon oregano leaves

4 plum tomatoes, skinned, deseeded and diced

16 black olives

350g (12oz) small new potatoes, peeled and thinly sliced

1/4 teaspoon saffron strands

4 large mackerel, cleaned and trimmed

150ml (1/4 pint) dry white wine

Juice of 2 lemons

Zest of 1 lemon, finely grated

Salt and freshly ground black pepper

JOHN DORY WITH MORELS, LEEKS, TRUFFLES AND POTATO SAUCE

A dish to serve when you want to push the boat out – it is expensive, but why not treat yourself occasionally? A good substitute for John Dory is Alaskan halibut.

Preheat the oven to 200°C/400°F/gas mark 6. Cook the potatoes in boiling salted water until tender, then drain. Mash until smooth and set aside.

Lightly butter a large baking dish, season the fish fillets and place in the dish. Bring the chicken stock to the boil in a pan, add the leeks and soaked morels and poach for 4–5 minutes, until tender. Remove from the pan with a slotted spoon and set aside. Add the milk to the stock and then pour this mixture over the fish. Cover with lightly buttered greaseproof paper and bake for 6–8 minutes, until the fish is just done. Remove from the oven and drain off the cooking liquid through a fine sieve into a clean pan. Add the mashed potato and cream and whisk until smooth. Cut 25g (1oz) of the butter into pieces and whisk them into the sauce a few at a time. Add the chives and season to taste.

Heat the remaining butter in a pan, add the leeks, morels and truffle slices and reheat gently, then season. To serve, place the fish in 4 soup plates. Pour over the potato sauce and scatter the leek mixture on top.

175g (6oz) salad potatoes, such as Jersey Royal, Charlotte or La Ratte, peeled

4 x 175g (6oz) John Dory fillets (or other firm white fish)

100ml (3½ fl oz) chicken stock

20 young leeks, cut into 7.5cm (3in) lengths

10g (¼ oz) small dried morel mushrooms, soaked in hot water for 30 minutes and then drained

200ml (7fl oz) full-fat milk

100ml (3½ fl oz) single cream

50g (2oz) cold unsalted butter

1 tablespoon chopped chives

1 fresh or canned black truffle, thinly sliced

Salt and freshly ground black pepper

potato, courgette and king prawn spiedini with mustard-smoked paprika mayo

tip

TO SHELL AND DE-VEIN PRAWNS, twist off and discard the head if it is still attached, then break the shell open along the belly and carefully peel it off. Run the tip of a sharp knife along the back of the prawn and lift out the black intestinal vein.

Soak 4 bamboo skewers in cold water for up to 1 hour (this helps prevent them burning on the grill). Meanwhile, cook the potatoes in their skins in boiling salted water until just tender (they should still be slightly firm). Drain and leave to cool, then cut in half.

In a bowl, whisk together the mustard, balsamic vinegar, oil, basil and lemon juice. Drain the bamboo skewers and alternately thread onto them the courgettes, prawns and potatoes. Place in a shallow dish, season with salt and pepper, then pour over the marinade and leave at room temperature for 2–3 hours. Meanwhile, mix together all the ingredients for the mayonnaise and season to taste.

Brush a ridged grill pan with a little extra oil and heat until very hot. Cook the skewers on it, turning frequently, for 8–10 minutes, until the prawns and vegetables are charred and tender. Serve hot with the mustard-smoked paprika mayonnaise.

400g (14oz) small new potatoes

2 teaspoons Dijon mustard

3 tablespoons balsamic vinegar

3 tablespoons olive oil

10 basil leaves, torn

1 tablespoon lemon juice

3 courgettes, cut into slices 1cm (1/2 in) thick

20 large raw king prawns, shelled and de-veined (see Tip)

Salt and freshly ground black pepper

For the mustard–smoked paprika mayo:

150ml (1/4 pint) good-quality mayonnaise

1 tablespoon smoked paprika

1 teaspoon grain mustard

Juice of 1/2 lemon

1 garlic clove, crushed

potato and fennel seed crusted sea bass

Sea bass and fennel have always had a great affinity. This crisp, fennel-flavoured potato crust is perfect with the soft-textured bass.

Preheat the oven to 200°C/400°F/gas mark 6. Bake the potatoes until nearly cooked, then remove and leave to cool. Peel them and grate into a bowl, using the coarse slice of the grater. Add the garlic and toasted fennel seeds and season well.

Lightly beat together the milk and egg yolks. Season the fish with salt and pepper, then dip the top side of each fillet into the egg and milk. Dredge the top with the potato and fennel seed mixture, patting it on to ensure it sticks to the fish.

For the dressing, put the mustard, lemon juice and vinegar in a bowl and whisk in the olive oil. Add all the remaining ingredients, then transfer to a pan and heat gently.

Heat some olive oil in a large frying pan. When very hot, add the sea bass crust-side down and fry for 1–2 minutes, until golden. Reduce the heat and cook for a further 1–3 minutes, then turn over and cook the other side.

Briefly reheat the cooked asparagus tips in the butter and season to taste. Arrange on serving plates, top with the potato-crusted sea bass and pour the warm dressing around.

2 large waxy potatoes

1 small garlic clove, crushed

2 teaspoons fennel seeds, toasted briefly in a dry frying pan

100ml (3^1/$_2$ fl oz) full-fat milk

2 egg yolks

4 x 175g (6oz) thick sea bass fillets, skinned

Olive oil, for frying

20 freshly cooked asparagus tips

25g (1oz) unsalted butter

Salt and freshly ground black pepper

For the dressing:

^{1}/$_2$ teaspoon Dijon mustard

1 tablespoon lemon juice

1 tablespoon champagne vinegar

4 tablespoons olive oil

1 shallot, finely chopped

8 black olives, pitted and chopped

1 tablespoon chopped chives

2 plum tomatoes, skinned, deseeded and chopped

BRIXHAM fish pie

During my time on the 'This Morning' programme with Richard and Judy, I prepared this fish pie for a feature on basic British cooking. It was a great hit, especially with the camera crew who took no time at all to devour it.

Put the potatoes in a pan, cover with water, add a little salt and bring to the boil. Reduce the heat and simmer until just tender, then drain in a colander and return to the pan. With a fork, lightly crush the potatoes, keeping them fairly chunky. Stir in 25g (1oz) of the butter and season to taste, then set aside.

Place the salmon and cod in a wide, deep pan, pour over the milk and add the bay leaf and a few dill stalks. Bring to the boil, then reduce the heat and simmer for 3–4 minutes. Add the scallops and cook for a further minute. Remove all the fish with a slotted spoon. Strain the cooking liquid and set aside. Flake the cod and salmon into large pieces and place in a buttered 1.2 litre (2 pint) casserole dish with the scallops.

Preheat the oven to 200°C/400°F/gas mark 6. Melt the remaining butter in a pan, add the onion and cook over a low heat until tender. Stir in the flour and cook for 1 minute. Remove from the heat and gradually stir in the reserved milk to form a sauce, then return to the heat and bring to the boil, stirring constantly. Simmer for 5 minutes, then add the cream and reheat gently. Stir in the chopped dill and prawns, season to taste and pour the sauce over the fish. Scatter the crushed potatoes on top until the fish is covered completely. Sprinkle over the cheese and bake for 20–25 minutes, until the potatoes are golden and the sauce is bubbling.

- 900g (2lb) floury potatoes, peeled and cut into chunks
- 75g (3oz) unsalted butter
- 225g (8oz) salmon fillet, skinned
- 225g (8oz) cod fillet, skinned
- 600ml (1 pint) full-fat milk
- 1 bay leaf
- 2 tablespoons chopped dill (plus a few stalks)
- 6 fresh shelled scallops, cut horizontally in half
- 1 onion, chopped
- 50g (2oz) plain flour
- 300ml (1/2 pint) double cream
- 125g (4 1/2 oz) small cooked peeled prawns
- 100g (4oz) Cheddar cheese, grated
- Salt and freshly ground black pepper

fish cakes with tartare mousseline

I don't make fish cakes very often, perhaps because when I was at school they seemed to appear every day for lunch. However, when made well they can be excellent. Here's a great recipe with a good balance of potato and fish. The tartare sauce is finished with a little whipped cream to lighten it.

For the tartare sauce, stir the shallots, gherkins, capers, mustard and some salt and pepper into the mayonnaise, then fold in the whipped cream. Keep in the fridge until ready to serve.

Place the mashed potatoes in a large bowl. Flake the cooked salmon and add to the potatoes with the prawns. Season with cayenne, salt and pepper, then mix in the herbs and egg yolk. Turn the mixture out onto a floured surface and divide into 8 balls. Coat them in the flour, then dip into the beaten egg and finally coat with the crumbs.

Heat some vegetable oil to 180°C/350°F in a deep-fat fryer or a deep saucepan and fry the fish cakes for 3–4 minutes, until golden and crisp. Drain well on kitchen paper and serve with the creamy tartare mousseline and some lemon wedges.

tip

PANKO CRUMBS are dried breadcrumbs used in oriental cooking, especially for deep-frying. If you can find them (try Japanese and other oriental food shops), they give a fantastic crisp texture. Otherwise, ordinary dried white breadcrumbs can be substituted.

250g (9oz) mashed potato (made without any butter, milk or cream)

400g (14oz) salmon fillet, cooked and skinned

100g (4oz) small cooked peeled prawns

Cayenne pepper

2 tablespoons chopped mixed herbs, such as dill, parsley and chives

1 large egg yolk

Plain flour, for dusting

2 eggs, lightly beaten

150g (5oz) panko breadcrumbs (see Tip) or fresh white breadcrumbs (see Tip on page 86)

Vegetable oil, for deep-frying

Salt and freshly ground black pepper

Lemon wedges, to serve

For the tartare mousseline:

2 shallots, finely chopped

1 tablespoon finely chopped cocktail gherkins

1 tablespoon superfine capers, rinsed and drained

1/2 teaspoon Dijon mustard

100ml (3 1/2 fl oz) good-quality mayonnaise

4 tablespoons double cream, semi-whipped

baked sea bream on potato and fennel boulangère

This recipe is play on the classic potato boulangère, where sliced potatoes and onions are baked in a flavourful stock. Here I add thinly sliced fennel, which goes particularly well with this most delicate of fish. Salsa verde makes a good accompaniment.

Preheat the oven to 200°C/400°F/gas mark 6. Heat 2 tablespoons of the olive oil in a pan, add the fennel and onion and cook over a low heat until soft and pale golden.

Lightly rub an earthenware casserole with a little oil. Arrange a layer of potatoes over the base, season with salt and pepper and top with the fennel mixture. Arrange the remaining potatoes attractively on top in an overlapping layer, season then pour over the chicken stock so the vegetables are just covered. Dot the surface with the butter and bake for 30 minutes, until golden and crusty.

Remove the boulangère from the oven, season the fish and place it on top of the potatoes. Drizzle over the remaining olive oil, then return to the oven for 8–10 minutes, until the fish is done.

4 tablespoons olive oil

2 large fennel bulbs, thinly sliced

1 onion, thinly sliced

600g (1lb 5oz) waxy potatoes, peeled and cut into slices about 3mm (1/8 in) thick

750ml (1 1/4 pints) chicken stock

25g (1oz) unsalted butter, cut into small pieces

4 x 150g (5oz) sea bream (or Arctic char) fillets

Coarse sea salt and freshly ground black pepper

ROASTED TURBOT WITH PANCETTA, SQUID AND POTATO RISOTTO

This unusual risotto substitutes potatoes for the rice. The squid is wrapped in pancetta, which helps keep it moist and tender.

Using a mandolin or a large knife, cut the potatoes into tiny cubes slightly larger than rice grains, placing them in cold water as you go. Cook the peas in boiling salted water, then drain, refresh under cold running water and set aside. Heat half the olive oil in a pan, add the shallots, thyme leaves and garlic and sauté over a low heat for 2–3 minutes. Drain the potatoes well and dry in a clean cloth. Add them to the shallots and sauté until opaque. Stir in the chicken stock a little at a time until all the liquid has been absorbed and the potatoes are cooked through. This should take about 15–20 minutes; do not let the potatoes become mushy. Add the cream, Parmesan and cooked peas and season to taste. Keep warm.

Preheat the oven to 200°C/400°F/gas mark 6. Shred the squid lengthways into strips about 5mm (1/4 in) thick. Divide into 4 portions and wrap each portion in a slice of pancetta. Heat the butter and the remaining oil in a large ovenproof frying pan. Season the turbot and the squid parcels, place in the pan and cook briefly until browned on both sides. Transfer to the oven, adding the sprigs of thyme for garnish to the pan, and roast for about 3–4 minutes, until the fish is just cooked through. Remove from the oven and keep warm.

For the sauce, place the vinegar, shallots, thyme and bay leaf in a pan and bring to the boil. Add the red wine and boil until almost completely evaporated, then add the stock and boil until the sauce has reduced and thickened enough to coat the back of a spoon.

Arrange the potato risotto on 4 plates. Top with the roasted turbot, then with the pancetta-wrapped squid. Pour the red wine sauce around, garnish with the thyme and serve.

350g (12oz) large new potatoes, peeled

100g (4oz) fresh or frozen peas

4 tablespoons olive oil

2 shallots, finely chopped

Leaves from 1 sprig of thyme, plus 4 sprigs
    of thyme to garnish

1 garlic clove, crushed

425ml (14fl oz) chicken stock

4 tablespoons double cream

25g (1oz) Parmesan cheese, freshly grated

2 large squid, cleaned

4 large, thin slices of pancetta, weighing
    about 100g (4oz) in total

50g (2oz) unsalted butter

4 x 175g (6oz) turbot fillets (alternatively,
    use cod or Alaskan halibut)

Salt and freshly ground black pepper

For the red wine sauce:

5 tablespoons red wine vinegar

2 shallots, chopped

A sprig of thyme

1 bay leaf

150ml (1/4 pint) red wine

300ml (1/2 pint) meat stock

garlic braised chicken with Lemon and rosemary potatoes and olives

tip

IN ORDER FOR THE SAUCE TO FORM A GLAZE, you need to use good gelatinous stock in this recipe. Either buy one of the tubs of fresh stock now available in most large supermarkets or use home-made stock.

Preheat the oven to 200°C/400°F/gas mark 6. Heat the olive oil and butter in a large ovenproof frying pan or a heavy-duty roasting tin. Add the chicken pieces in a single layer, then add the whole garlic cloves and the bay leaf and cook for 8–10 minutes, until coloured all over. Cover with foil, transfer to the oven and bake for 25 minutes. Meanwhile, cook the potatoes in boiling salted water for 8–10 minutes, until just tender. Drain and cut into wedges 2.5cm (1in) thick.

Add the wine to the pan and stir to coat the chicken pieces in it, then add the potatoes, rosemary, lemon zest, olives, stock and some seasoning and return to the oven, uncovered, for 15 minutes, until the sauce has formed a glaze around the chicken. Remove from the oven, add the balsamic vinegar and toss together, then serve.

4 tablespoons olive oil

25g (1oz) unsalted butter

12 small chicken joints

12 garlic cloves, peeled but left whole

1 bay leaf

275g (10oz) small waxy potatoes, peeled

5 tablespoons dry white wine

$^{1}/_{2}$ tablespoon roughly chopped rosemary

Zest of 1 lemon, finely grated

12 green olives

200ml (7fl oz) good-quality chicken stock

2 tablespoons balsamic vinegar

pan-roasted pork chops with spicy stewed potatoes and chorizo

Chorizo is a wonderful spicy sausage from Spain, available also in a smoked variety that I think has an unbeatable flavour. In this recipe, the spicy, smoky flavour permeates the whole dish.

Heat half the oil in a large frying pan until smoking, season the pork chops and seal in the hot oil until golden on both sides. Remove and set aside. Heat the remaining oil in the pan, add the onion, garlic and green pepper and fry for 2–3 minutes, until they begin to soften. Add the chorizo and cook for a couple of minutes more. Then add the whole unpeeled potatoes, bay leaf, saffron and harissa and cover with the chicken stock. Bring to the boil. Return the chops to the pan, then reduce the heat, cover and cook for 20–25 minutes, until the pork and potatoes are done and the sauce has thickened. Stir in the black olives and serve.

2 tablespoons vegetable oil

4 x 175g (6oz) pork chops

1 onion, finely chopped

1 garlic clove, crushed

1 green pepper, deseeded and chopped

75g (3oz) smoked chorizo sausage, thinly sliced

300g (11oz) Jersey Royals (or other small new potatoes)

1 bay leaf

^{1}/4 teaspoon saffron strands

1 tablespoon harissa paste

450ml (^{3}/4 pint) chicken stock

8 black olives

Salt and freshly ground black pepper

slow-cooked pork with sweet potatoes, tomatoes, basil and chillies

Sweet potatoes go very well with tomatoes and spices, while slow-cooking the pork gives it a wonderful texture and helps it retain its natural juices.

Cut the pork into 4 pieces, season with salt and pepper and place in an ovenproof dish. In a blender, blitz together the cumin seeds, half the garlic and 100ml (3¹/2 fl oz) of the olive oil. Pour this mixture over the pork, cover with foil and leave in the fridge overnight to marinate.

The next day, preheat the oven to 180°C/350°F/gas mark 4. Uncover the pork belly, place in the oven and cook for 30 minutes, until golden. Cover with foil again and return to the oven for a further 1–1¹/2 hours, until very tender.

Place the sweet potatoes and tomatoes in a roasting tin, drizzle with the remaining olive oil and roast for 40–45 minutes, until tender.

For the sauce, mix the grapeseed oil with the remaining garlic, the chillies, basil, ketjap manis, mirin and chicken stock and season to taste. Bring to the boil in a pan.

To serve, arrange the potatoes and tomatoes on individual serving plates. Cut the pork into slices 5mm (¹/4 in) thick and drape them over the potatoes, then drizzle over the basil and chilli dressing and serve.

900g (2lb) pork belly, rind and bone removed

¹/2 teaspoon cumin seeds, toasted briefly in a dry frying pan

2 garlic cloves, crushed

160ml (5¹/2 fl oz) olive oil

4 orange-fleshed sweet potatoes, peeled and cut into 2.5cm (1in) dice

2 white-fleshed sweet potatoes, peeled and cut into 2.5cm (1in) dice

6 plum tomatoes, cut lengthways in half

90ml (3fl oz) grapeseed oil

2 red chillies, deseeded and thinly sliced

10 basil leaves, chopped

2 tablespoons ketjap manis (Indonesian soy sauce)

2 tablespoons mirin (Japanese sweet rice wine)

100ml (3¹/2 fl oz) chicken stock

Coarse salt and freshly ground black pepper

sausages with caramelised truffle potatoes, red onions and garlic

A comforting meal that makes a change from the usual sausage and mash. The balsamic vinegar and wine sauce gives the sausages a delicious sweet aftertaste.

Preheat the oven to 190°C/375°F/gas mark 5. Cook the truffle potatoes in their skins in a pan of boiling salted water until tender, then drain, refresh under cold water and peel them while warm. Cut them in half lengthways and set aside.

Cut the red onions into wedges, leaving the root intact. Place the red onions, potato halves and garlic cloves in a roasting tin, pour over 6 tablespoons of the olive oil and the balsamic vinegar, then add the sugar, sage and thyme. Roast in the oven for about 30 minutes, until tender and caramelised.

Meanwhile, heat the remaining oil in a frying pan, add the sausages and cook for 10–12 minutes, until browned all over. Add them to the roasting tin, pour over the red wine and stock, season, and cook for 10–15 minutes, until the sausages are done.

350g (12oz) truffle potatoes (black potatoes)

4 red onions

12 garlic cloves, unpeeled

8 tablespoons olive oil

4 tablespoons balsamic vinegar

2 tablespoons brown sugar

1 tablespoon roughly chopped sage

1 tablespoon thyme leaves

450g (1lb) best-quality pork sausages

150ml (¼ pint) red wine

150ml (¼ pint) meat stock

Salt and freshly ground black pepper

my favourite cottage pie

Heat the vegetable oil in a large pan until smoking, season the beef with salt and pepper, then add it to the pan and fry for 3–4 minutes, until browned (this is best done in 2 batches, so as not to overcrowd the pan). When each batch is sealed, transfer to a colander to drain off the excess fat.

Melt the butter in the pan, add the garlic, vegetables, bacon and herbs and cook for 3–4 minutes, until they begin to turn golden. Return the beef to the pan, add the tomato purée and mix thoroughly. Cook over a low heat for 2–3 minutes, then sprinkle over the flour, stir it in and cook for a further 2–3 minutes. Pour in the red wine and bring to the boil, stirring as you go. Finally add the hot stock and orange zest and stir to form a sauce. Tuck in the bay leaf, cover the pan and simmer for 1–1 1/2 hours (or cook it in the oven at 190°C/375°F/gas mark 5), until everything is tender and a thick sauce has formed around the meat.

Meanwhile boil the potatoes and parsnips separately until tender, then drain and mash them separately. Combine them in a bowl, stir in the egg yolks, cream, cheese and mustard and season to taste.

Transfer the beef mixture to an ovenproof dish and leave to cool. Preheat the oven to 190°C/375°F/gas mark 5. Cover the beef mixture with the potato and parsnip mash and bake for 30–35 minutes, until the top is a nice, crusty golden brown.

4 tablespoons vegetable oil

450g (1lb) finely minced lean beef

50g (2oz) unsalted butter

1 garlic clove, crushed

1 large carrot, finely chopped

1 onion, finely chopped

1 large parsnip, finely chopped

1 swede, finely chopped

150g (5oz) streaky bacon, chopped

Leaves from 1 sprig of rosemary, chopped

Leaves from 1 sprig of thyme, chopped

2 tablespoons tomato purée

50g (2oz) plain flour

150ml (1/4 pint) red wine

750ml (1 1/4 pints) hot beef stock

1 bay leaf

Zest of 1 orange, finely grated

Salt and freshly ground black pepper

For the potato crust:

450g (1lb) floury potatoes, peeled and cut into chunks

300g (11oz) parsnips, peeled and cut into chunks

2 egg yolks

100ml (3 1/2 fl oz) double cream

4 tablespoons grated Cheddar cheese

1/2 tablespoon Dijon mustard

Salt and freshly ground black pepper

DRY-SPICED NEW POTATO CURRY

TIP

TO CLARIFY BUTTER,
heat it gently in a
small pan until it
begins to boil, then
boil for 2 minutes (or
heat in a microwave
for 1 minute). Pour off
the butter through a
fine conical strainer or
a muslin-lined sieve,
leaving behind the
white, milky sediment.
Store in the fridge.

Cook the new potatoes in boiling salted water for 10 minutes, then drain well and set aside. In a frying pan, dry-roast the cumin and fenugreek seeds for 1 minute, until fragrant. Remove from the pan and leave to cool, then grind them in a mortar or blender with a little water to form a paste. Heat half the ghee or clarified butter in a pan, add the onion and fry until lightly golden. Add the remaining ghee or clarified butter, then add the curry leaves and mustard seeds and fry for 30 seconds. Stir in the paste and cook for 2–3 minutes. Add the potatoes, turmeric, desiccated coconut, red chillies and enough water to half cover the ingredients. Cover the pan and cook gently for 8–10 minutes. Serve with fluffy plain boiled rice, preferably basmati.

650g (1lb 6oz) new potatoes, peeled

1 tablespoon cumin seeds

1 teaspoon fenugreek seeds

4 tablespoons ghee or clarified butter
   (see Tip)

1 onion, chopped

8 fresh curry leaves

2 teaspoons black mustard seeds

1 teaspoon turmeric

4 tablespoons unsweetened desiccated
   coconut

2 red chillies, deseeded and chopped

Salt and freshly ground black pepper

IRISH STEW

I once worked with an Irish chef who insisted that potatoes should be the only vegetable in this dish. Well, being English, I have decided to express a little poetic licence and add carrots, celery, parsnip and thyme to this renowned stew.

Arrange a layer of the lamb in a deep saucepan. Follow with a layer of onions, carrots, celery and parsnip, then season lightly. Sprinkle over half the thyme and some of the parsley, then cover with a layer of potatoes. Top with the remaining meat, followed by the vegetables, seasoning and herbs (reserve a little parsley for garnish), then add a final layer of potatoes.

Pour over the stock and bring to the boil. Cover with a lid or foil and simmer gently for 1¹/2–2 hours (or place in a low oven). Fat from the lamb will be released to the surface, so it may be necessary to skim off a little fat as it cooks. When the stew is ready, the meat and vegetables should be tender and some of the liquid should have been absorbed by the potatoes. Sprinkle over the remaining parsley before serving.

900g (2lb) neck end of lamb, cut into chops

3 onions, thinly sliced

2 carrots, sliced

2 celery sticks, sliced

1 parsnip, sliced

1 teaspoon thyme leaves

2 tablespoons chopped parsley

750g (1lb 10oz) floury potatoes, peeled
   and sliced

600ml (1 pint) lamb or other meat stock
   (or water)

Salt and freshly ground black pepper

Lamb and potato hotpot

A hearty comfort food if ever there was one. This hotpot takes me back to my childhood, when it made a regular appearance on our dinner table. It originates from Lancashire, where some of the best black pudding in Britain is made, and is sometimes known as tattie pot. Serve with pickled red cabbage.

Preheat the oven to 190°C/375°F/gas mark 5. Trim excess fat from the lamb chops and remove the skin and central core from the kidneys.

Heat the lard in a heavy-based casserole, add the lamb chops and fry for 2–3 minutes, until well-sealed and golden on both sides. Remove and set aside. Add the kidneys and black pudding and seal them on both sides, then remove from the pan.

Add the onions and half the thyme to the casserole and fry for 4–5 minutes, until golden. Place the meat on top, starting with the lamb, then the kidneys and finally the black pudding. Arrange the potatoes in overlapping slices over the black pudding, seasoning with salt and pepper as you go. Sprinkle over the remaining thyme leaves.

Pour over the hot stock so that the potatoes are just covered, add a final seasoning, then dot the top of the potatoes with the butter. Cover the casserole, transfer to the oven and bake for 1–1¼ hours. Remove the lid and bake for a further 30 minutes to crisp up the potatoes and give them a lovely golden colour.

8 middle-neck lamb chops

4 lamb's kidneys

2 tablespoons lard (or vegetable oil)

2 black puddings, cut into slices 5mm (¼ in) thick

2 onions, thinly sliced

1 tablespoon thyme leaves

675g (1½ lb) baking potatoes, peeled and thinly sliced

750ml (1¼ pints) hot meat stock

25g (1oz) unsalted butter

Coarse salt and freshly ground black pepper

sweet potato Laksa

A really satisfying noodle soup from Indonesia and Malaysia. There are many recipes for laksa, using chicken, fish or prawns, but this one is ideal for vegetarians. The list of ingredients may look long but it is simple to prepare.

Heat 1 tablespoon of the oil in a large pan, add the beancurd and fry until golden and crisp. Remove from the pan and set aside.

Heat the remaining oil in the pan, add the onion and garlic and cook over a medium heat until softened. Add the sweet potatoes and toss with the onion and garlic. Stir in the ground macadamia nuts, cumin, coriander, half the chilli and the blachan and cook for 2 minutes. Add the curry paste and cook for 5 minutes to release the fragrance. Stir in the stock and bring to the boil, then add the coconut milk, sugar and lime zest, reduce the heat to a simmer and cook for 10 minutes.

Cook the rice noodles in boiling water for 5 minutes and then drain. Place them in 4 deep soup bowls and top with the fried beancurd. Stir the beansprouts into the soup, season to tase, and pour over the noodles. Sprinkle the spring onions, coriander, mint and remaining chilli on top, and serve.

3 tablespoons groundnut or vegetable oil

200g (7oz) pressed beancurd, cut into 1cm ($1/2$ in) cubes

1 onion, finely chopped

2 garlic cloves, crushed

350g (12oz) orange-fleshed sweet potatoes, peeled and cut into 1cm ($1/2$ in) cubes

25g (1oz) macadamia nuts, ground

1 teaspoon ground cumin

1 teaspoon ground coriander

2 small red chillies, deseeded and thinly sliced

$1/2$ teaspoon blachan (shrimp paste)

$1^{1}/2$ tablespoons yellow (or red) Thai curry paste

300ml ($1/2$ pint) vegetable (or chicken) stock

600ml (1 pint) coconut milk

1 tablespoon brown sugar

Zest of 1 lime, finely grated

250g (9oz) flat rice noodles

200g (7oz) beansprouts

4 spring onions, shredded

1 tablespoon chopped coriander

1 tablespoon chopped mint

Salt and freshly ground black pepper

Here are several of my favourite sauces for giving a kick to simply boiled or steamed potatoes. The potatoes and their sauce can be served as an accompaniment to plain roast or grilled meat or fish – although many of them are delicious enough to be served as a dish in their own right.

sauces for boiled potatoes

camembert cheese fondue

1 garlic clove, peeled

200g (7oz) ripe Camembert cheese, rind removed

2 tablespoons crème fraîche

1 tablespoon kirsch

2 tablespoons chopped chives (optional)

Rub the inside of a small pan with the garlic clove. Place the cheese and crème fraîche in the pan and heat very gently until the cheese has melted. Stir in the kirsch and the chives, if using, and pour over hot potatoes.

baked potato, buttermilk and herb dressing

1 large floury potato

1 tablespoon Dijon mustard

1 garlic clove, crushed

1 tablespoon olive oil

3 tablespoons white wine vinegar

Buttermilk

3 tablespoons chopped mixed herbs, such as chives, basil, parsley and tarragon

Pinch of sugar

Salt and freshly ground black pepper

Bake the potato until tender (see page 70), then cut it in half and scoop out the flesh into a blender. Blitz with the mustard, garlic, oil, vinegar and enough buttermilk to give a smooth, creamy consistency, similar to single cream. Pour into a bowl and stir in the herbs, a good pinch of sugar and seasoning to taste. Pour over hot potatoes and serve.

shallot mustard soubise

15g (^{1}/$_2$ oz) unsalted butter

6 shallots, finely chopped

5 tablespoons dry white wine

150ml (^{1}/$_4$ pint) chicken stock

100ml (3^1/$_2$ fl oz) double cream

2 tablespoons chopped parsley

1 tablespoon wholegrain mustard

Salt and freshly ground black pepper

Heat the butter in a small pan, add the shallots and sweat for 5–8 minutes, until softened but not coloured. Add the wine and simmer until it has completely evaporated. Pour in the chicken stock and simmer until reduced by half. Finally add the cream and simmer until reduced by half again. Pour the sauce into a blender and blitz to a purée, then pour into a pan, reheat gently and stir in the parsley and mustard. Season to taste, pour over hot potatoes and serve.

tip

ALWAYS ADD MUSTARD to sauces at the last minute and don't allow it to boil, otherwise the flavour will become bitter.

soured cream, capers and watercress

2 bunches of watercress

4 tablespoons soured cream

1 tablespoon baby capers, rinsed and
    drained

1 teaspoon finely grated lemon zest

Salt and freshly ground black pepper

Remove the stalks from the watercress and chop the leaves. Mix the watercress, soured cream, capers and seasoning together, pour over the hot potatoes and sprinkle with grated lemon zest.

saffron gribiche dressing

1 teaspoon Dijon mustard

1 tablespoon white wine vinegar

100ml (3^1/$_2$ fl oz) olive oil

A pinch of saffron strands, steeped in 2
    tablespoons boiling water

1 tablespoon lemon juice

2 shallots, finely chopped

2 tablespoons baby capers, rinsed and
    drained

2 eggs, hard-boiled and roughly chopped

1 tablespoon chopped parsley

Salt and freshly ground black pepper

Whisk together the mustard, vinegar and oil. Add the saffron liquid, lemon juice, shallots, capers, hard-boiled eggs and parsley and mix well together. Season to taste and pour over hot potatoes.

ocopa

This Peruvian sauce, whose name dates back to the Incas, is a speciality of Lima. The recipe was given to me by a Peruvian friend who now lives in London. It is usually served as an appetiser.

125g (4^1/$_2$ oz) quinoa

4 tablespoons olive oil

1 onion, finely chopped

1 jalapeño chilli, chopped

2 garlic cloves, crushed

1 teaspoon ground cumin

2 tablespoons light soy sauce

75g (3oz) hard cheese, such as Cheddar,
    grated

2 tablespoons chopped parsley

200ml (7fl oz) full-fat milk

Green olives and slices of hard-boiled egg,
    to garnish

Salt and freshly ground black pepper

Heat a dry frying pan, add the quinoa and dry-fry for 1–2 minutes, until lightly toasted. Pour in just enough water to cover, bring to the boil, then reduce the heat and simmer for 10–15 minutes, until the quinoa is tender and has absorbed all the water.

Meanwhile, heat half the oil in a separate frying pan, add the onion and cook for 8–10 minutes, until softened. Stir in half the chilli, the garlic, cumin, soy sauce and some salt and pepper. Cook for a couple of minutes, then remove from the heat and leave to cool.

Put the onion mixture in a blender with the remaining chilli and oil, plus the cheese, parsley, quinoa and milk and blitz to a paste. Pour this sauce over hot new potatoes and garnish with green olives and slices of hard-boiled egg.

jersey royals with butter and mint

Here is a perfect example of the virtues of simplicity. Jersey Royals are one of the great tastes of summer. Until recently I was involved in the Good Food Festival in Jersey every April and May. This is when the first Jersey Royals are harvested, and what a treat they are. My fellow judges and I always looked forward to tasting them as much as to the festival itself. They are grown exclusively in Jersey, since strangely enough they seem to be unsuccessful anywhere else. Nothing beats their slightly sweet taste and creamy texture – it's as if the butter was grown inside them. They are at their best simply boiled or steamed, then topped with butter and mint, and no book of potato recipes would be complete without their inclusion.

A small handful of mint
900g (2lb) Jersey Royals, scrubbed
75g (3oz) unsalted butter
Salt and freshly ground black pepper

Bring a pan of salted water to the boil. Remove the stalks from the mint and add to the pan with the potatoes. Simmer for 10–20 minutes, until the potatoes are tender.

Meanwhile, chop the mint leaves and beat them with the butter in a bowl. Drain the potatoes in a colander, then place them in a serving bowl. Season to taste, top with the mint butter and serve.

salmorreta sauce

This sauce can be blitzed to a smooth purée, or combined roughly for a chunkier presentation

350g (12oz) ripe but firm plum tomatoes, cut in half
$^1/_2$ teaspoon red chilli flakes
2 garlic cloves, chopped
1 tablespoon chopped parsley
1 tablespoon chopped tarragon
1 red onion, finely chopped
About 100ml ($3^1/_2$ fl oz) olive oil
2 tablespoons white wine vinegar
A pinch of sugar
Salt and freshly ground black pepper

Put the tomatoes on a baking tray in a single layer and place under a hot grill for 3–4 minutes on each side, until slightly charred. Carefully peel off the skin and discard the pips.

Put the chilli flakes, garlic, parsley and tarragon in a mortar and crush. Add the onion and the tomato flesh and crush again. Drizzle in enough olive oil to give a pesto-like consistency, stirring constantly, then add the vinegar and sugar. Season to taste. Pour over hot potatoes to serve.

hot paprika and almond dressing

1 garlic clove, chopped
40g ($1^1/_2$ oz) whole blanched almonds
$^1/_4$ teaspoon cayenne pepper
$^1/_4$ teaspoon hot paprika (or chilli powder)
1 tablespoon sherry vinegar
4 tablespoons olive oil
1 tablespoon chopped parsley
1 tablespoon chopped oregano
Salt

Whizz the garlic and almonds to a fine paste in a small food processor (or crush them in a mortar if you are feeling energetic). Transfer to a bowl and mix in the cayenne and paprika. Stir in the vinegar and olive oil, followed by the herbs, then season with a little salt. Pour over hot potatoes and serve.

potatoes are so adaptable that they can even be used in puddings. They add lightness and moisture to all sorts of sweet dishes, and can replace suet or a proportion of the flour in steamed and baked puddings, pastry and some cakes. Orange-fleshed sweet potatoes, with their honeyed, almost caramelised flavour, are a natural when it comes to desserts. Don't be tempted to substitute white-fleshed sweet potatoes, though – their taste and texture are not the same at all.

This chapter contains just a few ideas for potato puddings but gives a fair indication of their versatility. Chunky Orange Marmalade Tart (page 164) includes a little mashed potato in the pastry for a light, soft texture. Stuffed Almond Pancakes with Peach Brandy Sabayon (page 173) rely on potatoes to produce delicate, thin crêpes. And grated potato is the secret ingredient in Steamed Lemon and Apricot Pudding (page 171). Other recipes, such as Cuban Bread Pudding (page 166), are based on potato bread. Ordinary bread can be substituted but potato bread has a unique flavour and texture that add an indefinable quality to these dishes – it would always be my first choice for making them.

a few
sweet
IDEAS

chunky orange marmalade tart

Rich and gooey in texture, this tart takes me back to my schooldays with great affection.

For the pastry, sift the flour and salt into a bowl and mix in the mashed potato. Rub in the butter with your fingertips until the mixture resembles crumbs, then bring together into a dough, adding a little cold water to bind if necessary. Wrap in clingfilm and chill for 1 hour.

Preheat the oven to 200°C/400°F/gas mark 6. Roll out the pastry and use to line a lightly greased 20–23cm (8–9in) tart tin, trimming the edges neatly. Put the orange marmalade in a pan with the butter and heat gently until the butter has melted, then stir in the vanilla extract, lemon zest and juice. Lightly beat the eggs in a bowl, pour in the warm orange marmalade and mix well. Pour the mixture into the pastry case and bake for 20–25 minutes. Leave to cool before serving. The filling will firm up as it cools.

100g (4oz) self-raising flour

A pinch of salt

50g (2oz) mashed potato (made without any butter, milk or cream)

75g (3oz) unsalted butter, cut into small pieces

For the filling:

300ml (1/2 pint) chunky orange marmalade

50g (2oz) unsalted butter

Juice and finely grated zest of 1 lemon

1/2 teaspoon vanilla extract

2 eggs

sweet potato and apple clafoutis

A simple, satisfying and unusual dessert, ideal for a cold winter's evening. I like it topped with a scoop of vanilla ice-cream.

Put the sweet potatoes in a pan, cover with cold water and bring to the boil. Reduce the heat and simmer until just tender, then drain. When the potatoes are cool enough to handle, peel them and cut into 1cm (1/2 in) cubes.

Preheat the oven to 190°C/375°F/gas mark 5. Melt the butter in a large frying pan, stir in the sugar and cook over a medium heat until lightly caramelised. Add the apple wedges and sweet potatoes and cook until caramelised and golden. Add the Calvados, heat for a few seconds, then flambé by setting light to it, standing well back. When the flames have died down, use a slotted spoon to transfer the apples and sweet potatoes to a lightly greased ovenproof dish, approximately 23 x 15cm (9 x 6in).

For the batter, put the eggs and sugar in a bowl and whisk until creamy. Sift in the flour and a little pinch of salt and whisk until smooth. Put the milk, cream and vanilla in a pan and bring to the boil, then pour onto the egg mixture, whisking until smooth. Whisk in the Calvados and pour the batter over the apples and potatoes. Bake for 20–25 minutes, until just set. Remove from the oven and cool slightly. Sprinkle with icing sugar and serve.

300g (11oz) orange-fleshed sweet potatoes

25g (1oz) unsalted butter

50g (2oz) caster sugar

300g (11oz) Granny Smith apples, peeled, cored and cut into thick wedges

4 tablespoons Calvados

Icing sugar, for dusting

For the batter:

4 eggs, lightly beaten

50g (2oz) caster sugar

25g (1oz) plain flour

A pinch of salt

120ml (4fl oz) full-fat milk

150ml (1/4 pint) whipping cream

2 drops of vanilla extract

4 tablespoons Calvados

CUBAN BREAD PUDDING WITH BANANAS AND RUM CARAMEL

A Cuban-inspired pudding made to a lighter recipe than the original. It is flavoured with coconut milk and sweet spices and topped with bananas and a rum caramel. Serve with lashings of thick cream if, like me, you don't count calories!

Preheat the oven to 160°C/325°F/gas mark 3. Lightly grease four 175ml (6fl oz) ramekin dishes. Divide the diced bread between the dishes and sprinkle over the soaked sultanas.

Put the cream, coconut milk, spices and almond essence in a pan. Slit open the vanilla pod and scrape out the seeds into the pan, then place over a gentle heat and bring just to the boil. Meanwhile, put the eggs and sugar in a bowl and whisk until pale. Strain the cream mixture and gradually pour it into the egg and sugar mixture, whisking constantly. Pour into the ramekins and leave to stand for 30 minutes. Place the dishes carefully in a roasting tin and pour enough boiling water into the tin to come halfway up the sides of the dishes. Bake for 20–25 minutes or until just set, then remove from the oven and allow to cool slightly.

For the rum caramel, spread the sugar over the base of a heavy pan and cook over a medium heat until melted, stirring gently from time to time so it melts evenly. Raise the heat and cook to a dark amber caramel. Cool slightly and stir in the rum.

Turn the puddings out of the ramekins and place on serving plates. Peel the bananas and cut into 5mm (1/4in) thick slices. Arrange the slices of banana on top and pour over the rum caramel.

5 slices of Potato Bread (see page 110), cut into 1cm (1/2 in) cubes

15g (1/2 oz) sultanas, soaked in hot water for 30 minutes and then drained

150ml (1/4 pint) double cream

350ml (12fl oz) unsweetened coconut milk

A small pinch of saffron strands

1/4 teaspoon ground cinnamon

A pinch of freshly grated nutmeg

1/4 teaspoon almond essence

1/2 vanilla pod

3 large eggs

125g (41/2 oz) caster sugar

2 small, ripe bananas

For the rum caramel:

100g (4oz) caster sugar

4 tablespoons dark rum

espresso and sweet potato tart

**YOU WILL ONLY
NEED about half
the pastry for
this recipe but
the rest can be
well wrapped
and stored in
the freezer.**

*This tart has a rich, creamy, coffee-flavoured filling. It's very good served
with chocolate sauce.*

First make the pastry. Sift the flour onto a work surface and make a
well in the centre. Put the butter, salt, sugar and lemon zest in the well
and then add the egg. With your fingertips, gradually bring the flour
into the centre, blending in the butter until all the ingredients come
together to form a soft dough. Knead lightly for 1 minute, until
smooth, then shape into a ball, cover with clingfilm and chill for 2 hours.

Preheat the oven to 180°C/350°F/gas mark 4. Roll out the pastry and
use to line a deep 20cm (8in) tart tin (see Tip). Line with greaseproof
paper, fill with baking beans and bake blind for 8–10 minutes, until the
pastry is quite dry. Remove the paper and beans and return the pastry
case to the oven for 5 minutes, then leave to cool. Leave the oven on.

For the filling, put the sweet potatoes in a pan, cover with cold water
and bring to the boil. Reduce the heat and simmer until tender, then
drain and leave until cool enough to handle. Peel the potatoes and
whizz to a purée in a blender, or push them through a sieve. Set aside.

Put the cream, milk, orange zest and juice and half the sugar in a pan
and bring to the boil. Stir in the espresso, remove from the heat and
cool slightly. Beat the eggs and egg yolks with the remaining sugar,
then slowly whisk in the warm coffee cream. Stir in the sweet potato
purée, blend well and pour into the pastry case. Place on a baking
sheet and cook for 40 minutes or until set. Leave to cool slightly, then
remove from the tart tin. Serve warm or cold.

250g (9oz) orange-fleshed sweet potatoes

300ml (1/2 pint) double cream

150ml (1/4 pint) full-fat milk

Juice and finely grated zest of 1 orange

50g (2oz) caster sugar

100ml (3 1/2 fl oz) strong espresso coffee

2 eggs

4 egg yolks

For the pastry:

350g (12oz) plain flour

225g (8oz) unsalted butter (at room
temperature), cut into small pieces

A pinch of salt

100g (4oz) icing sugar, sifted

Zest of 1/2 lemon, finely grated

1 egg, lightly beaten

caramelised apple french toast with peach jam

This is wonderful with double cream or a good scoop of vanilla ice-cream.

Slit the vanilla pod open and scrape out the seeds. Put them in a pan with the milk and cinnamon and bring to the boil, then pour into a shallow dish and leave to cool. Add the eggs, orange zest and caster sugar and whisk until smooth. Put the sliced bread in the egg mixture and leave to soak for 1 minute, then remove and drain.

Heat 25g (1oz) of the butter in a large frying pan, add the bread slices and fry for about 2 minutes on each side, until golden. Remove from the pan and keep warm. Add the brown sugar and the remaining butter to the pan and cook, stirring, for 2 minutes to form a light caramel. Add the apples and cook for 2–3 minutes on each side, until golden and tender. Pour over the wine, let it bubble for 30 seconds, then remove the pan from the heat.

Put the pieces of French toast on 4 serving plates, place a spoonful of peach jam on each one and top with a caramelised apple half. Dust with icing sugar and serve straight away.

1 vanilla pod

250ml (8fl oz) full-fat milk

1 teaspoon ground cinnamon

2 eggs

Juice and finely grated zest of 1 orange

100g (4oz) caster sugar

4 slices of Potato Bread (see page 110), cut
   2.5cm (1in) thick

40g (1¹/2 oz) unsalted butter

1 tablespoon brown sugar

2 Granny Smith apples, peeled, cored and
   cut horizontally in half

100ml (3¹/2 fl oz) dry white wine

4 tablespoons peach jam

Icing sugar, for dusting

deep-fried stuffed apricots

An unusual way of serving one of my favourite and most delicate of fruits. It's also a great way of using up leftover potato bread, should you have any!

Blanch the apricots in boiling water for 1 minute, then drain well and peel off the skins. Carefully cut down one side of each apricot and remove the stone, without damaging the flesh. In a bowl, mix together all the ingredients for the filling and use to stuff the apricots, closing them up afterwards.

Stir the orange zest into the Greek yoghurt and chill until ready to serve.

Mix together the breadcrumbs and ground almonds. Dip the stuffed apricots in the beaten eggs, then roll them in the breadcrumb mixture.

Heat some vegetable oil for deep-frying to 180°C/350°F and deep-fry the apricots for about 2 minutes, until golden – they will bob up to the surface, so keep pushing them down to allow them to colour evenly. Drain on kitchen paper and serve immediately, with the orange-scented yoghurt.

12 ripe apricots

1 teaspoon finely grated orange zest

100ml ($3^1/2$ fl oz) Greek yoghurt

125g ($4^1/2$ oz) fresh breadcrumbs, made from Potato Bread (see page 110)

50g (2oz) ground almonds

2 eggs, beaten

Vegetable oil, for deep-frying

For the filling:

12 fresh dates, stoned and roughly chopped

4 tablespoons ground almonds

Juice of $1/4$ lemon

Zest of 1 orange, finely grated

$1/2$ teaspoon ground cinnamon

1 tablespoon orange-flower water (optional)

2 tablespoons dark rum

steamed Lemon and apricot pudding

A fantastically warming winter pud, crammed with dried apricots and topped with apricot jam. Because the grated potato keeps it moist, it's surprisingly low in fat – unless you serve it with thick cream or lashings of custard sauce, as I do!

Sift the flour into a bowl, add the melted butter, then stir in all the remaining ingredients except the apricot jam. Transfer the mixture to a greased 900ml (1¹/₂ pint) pudding basin, cover with greaseproof paper or foil and tie with string to secure. Place the basin in a steamer or in a large pan containing enough boiling water to come halfway up the side of the basin. Cover and steam for 1¹/₄–1¹/₂ hours, topping up with more boiling water if necessary during cooking.

Remove from the pan and leave to cool for a few minutes, then take off the paper or foil and run a knife around the sides of the pudding to loosen it. Turn out onto a plate. Heat the jam with 100ml (3¹/₂ fl oz) water to form a sauce, then strain through a sieve. Pour it over the pudding and serve immediately.

50g (2oz) self-raising flour

50g (2oz) unsalted butter, melted

25g (1oz) caster sugar

1 tablespoon golden syrup

100g (4oz) soft white breadcrumbs

100g (4oz) grated raw potato

2 teaspoons finely grated lemon zest

100ml (3¹/₂ fl oz) full-fat milk

75g (3oz) dried apricots, chopped

175ml (6fl oz) apricot jam

Stuffed almond pancakes, waiting to be covered with brandy sauce and returned to the oven for glazing

stuffed almond pancakes with peach brandy sabayon

It's a great shame that pancakes are usually reserved for Shrove Tuesday, and rarely seen on menus. Here's one of my favourite ways to prepare them.

First make the pancakes. Put the potatoes in a pan, cover with cold water, add a pinch of salt and bring to the boil. Reduce the heat and simmer until tender, then drain well and mash to a purée. Leave to cool. Mix in the eggs, then sift in the flour, add the sugar and mix well. Gradually stir in enough milk to make a smooth, runny batter.

Heat some clarified butter in a 23cm (9in) non-stick frying pan, add a little of the batter and swirl it around the pan to coat the base thinly. Cook until golden underneath, then flip over and cook the other side. Make 8 pancakes in all, adding more butter to the pan as necessary.

For the filling, whisk the egg yolks and icing sugar together until creamy, then stir in the ground almonds and cinnamon. In a separate bowl, whisk the egg whites until stiff, then gradually whisk in the caster sugar. Gently fold the egg whites into the almond mixture. Divide the filling between the pancakes and roll them gently. Place on a large buttered baking sheet in pairs, leaving a good-sized gap in between.

Preheat the oven to 180°C/350°F/gas mark 4. For the sauce, place the egg yolks, sugar, wine or champagne and peach brandy in a large bowl and set it over a pan of barely simmering water, making sure the water isn't touching the base of the bowl. Whisk with a hand-held electric beater until the mixture becomes light and airy and increases by about four times its volume. Fold in the whipped cream.

Pour the sauce over the pancakes and place in the oven to glaze for 5 minutes. Meanwhile, heat the 15g (1/2 oz) butter in a large frying pan, add the caster sugar and cook until it forms a light caramel. Add the nectarine slices and cook until caramelised. Arrange the pancakes on 4 serving plates, garnish with the nectarines and dust with icing sugar.

2 egg yolks

1 tablespoon icing sugar, plus extra for dusting

75g (3oz) ground almonds

1/4 teaspoon ground cinnamon

2 egg whites

2 tablespoons caster sugar

15g (1/2 oz) unsalted butter

2 ripe but firm nectarines, stoned and thinly sliced

For the pancake batter:

250g (9oz) floury potatoes, peeled and cut into chunks

4 eggs

125g (4 1/2 oz) plain flour

1 tablespoon caster sugar

About 250ml (8fl oz) full-fat milk

25g (1oz) clarified butter (see Tip on page 153)

For the sauce:

3 egg yolks

75g (3oz) caster sugar

100ml (3 1/2 fl oz) sparkling white wine or champagne

4 tablespoons peach brandy

100ml (3 1/2 fl oz) double cream, semi-whipped

INDEX

acknowledgements

I gratefully acknowledge the assistance of the following people, without whom this book would not have been possible.

All at Kyle Cathie especially to Kyle, and to Sheila Boniface for her help and guidance.

Jane Middleton for another superb job of editing my recipes.

Linda Tubby and Gus Filgate, food stylist and photographer, between them they make a most talented and formidable pairing – thank you.

Penny Markham, for her wonderful props, once again.

Heidi Baker for her fantastic book design.

My wife, Anita, and daughter, Lauren, for their help and PC skills during the books initial concept.

Eddie from Laxeiro for inspiration from his wonderful Spanish recipes.

Alan Wilson, author of *The Story of the Potato*, whose help with detailed research has been invaluable.

Fiona, Linda and Honey at Limelight for their tireless support and friendship.

To all at Chef's Connection, vegetable purveyors, for supplying excellent quality potatoes and other wonderful produce to work with.

To Mr. Geoffrey Gelardi and my team at the Lanesborough for their constant support and encouragement during the writing of this book.